The Soteriological Use of Call
by Paul and Luke

Australian College of Theology Monograph Series

SERIES EDITOR GRAEME R. CHATFIELD

The ACT Monograph Series, generously supported by the Board of Directors of the Australian College of Theology, provides a forum for publishing quality research theses and studies by its graduates and affiliated college staff in the broad fields of Biblical Studies, Christian Thought and History, and Practical Theology with Wipf and Stock Publishers of Eugene, Oregon. The ACT selects the best of its doctoral and research masters theses as well as monographs that offer the academic community, scholars, church leaders and the wider community uniquely Australian and New Zealand perspectives on significant research topics and topics of current debate. The ACT also provides opportunity for contributors beyond its graduates and affiliated college staff to publish monographs which support the mission and values of the ACT.

Rev Dr Graeme Chatfield
Series Editor and Associate Dean

The Soteriological Use of Call
by Paul and Luke

IAN HUSSEY

WIPF & STOCK · Eugene, Oregon

THE SOTERIOLOGICAL USE OF CALL BY PAUL AND LUKE

Copyright © 2018 Ian Hussey. All rights reserved. Except for brief quotations in critical publications or reviews, no part of this book may be reproduced in any manner without prior written permission from the publisher. Write: Permissions, Wipf and Stock Publishers, 199 W. 8th Ave., Suite 3, Eugene, OR 97401.

Wipf & Stock
An Imprint of Wipf and Stock Publishers
199 W. 8th Ave., Suite 3
Eugene, OR 97401

www.wipfandstock.com

PAPERBACK ISBN: 978-1-5326-4900-4
HARDCOVER ISBN: 978-1-5326-4901-1
EBOOK ISBN: 978-1-5326-4902-8

Manufactured in the U.S.A.   06/28/18

Contents

Contents | v
Acknowledgements | vii
Abbreviations | viii

1 Introduction | 1
   1.1 Called or Invited? | 1
   1.2 The History of Scholarship on This Topic | 2
   1.2.1 Jesus and Paul | 2
   1.2.2 Luke and Paul | 3
   1.2.3 The Soteriologies of Luke and Paul | 4
   1.2.4 The Word καλέω | 8
   1.2.5 The Translation of καλέω | 11
   1.3 What You Need to Know About This Book | 13
   1.4 Why This Book Is Important | 16
   1.5 The Structure of This Book | 18

2 Old Testament Background | 19
   2.1 Introduction | 19
   2.2 The Call of Israel | 19
   2.3 Call and Election | 22
   2.4 Call and Covenant | 25
   2.5 The Covenant Meal | 29
   2.6 The Messianic Banquet | 31
   2.7 Summation | 33

3 The Soteriologies of Paul and Luke | 35
   3.1 Introduction | 35
   3.2 The Soteriology of Paul | 36

    3.2.1 Righteousness—A Metaphor of Salvation | 36
    3.2.2 Covenant Is an Important Part of Pauline Soteriology | 40
    3.2.3 Righteousness Is Related to Covenant Rather Than Imputation | 44
    3.2.4 Summation | 46
    3.3 The Soteriology of Luke | 46
    3.3.1 Salvation in Luke | 47
    3.3.2 Trajectories of Lukan Soteriology | 48
    3.3.3 Salvation and the Kingdom of God | 50
    3.3.4 Salvation and the Covenants | 52
    3.3.5 Summation | 58
    3.4 Chapter Summation | 58

4 Paul's Soteriological Use of Call | 60
    4.1 Introduction | 60
    4.2 Galatians 1:6 | 60
    4.4 Galatians 5:8 | 63
    4.5 Galatians 5:13 | 63
    4.6 1 Thessalonians 2:11–12 | 64
    4.7 1 Thessalonians 4:7 | 65
    4.8 1 Thessalonians 5:24 | 66
    4.9 2 Thessalonians 1:11 | 66
    4.10 2 Thessalonians 2:14 | 67
    4.11 1 Corinthians 1:2 | 68
    4.12 1 Corinthians 1:9 | 69
    4.13 1 Corinthians 1:26 | 70
    4.14 1 Corinthians 7:15–24 | 71
    4.15 Romans 1:6–7 | 73
    4.16 Romans 4:16–17 | 74
    4.17 Romans 8:28–30 | 75
    4.18 Romans 9:7 | 77
    4.19 Romans 9:10–13 | 78
    4.20 Romans 9:22–26 | 78
    4.21 Romans 11:28–29 | 80
    4.22 Ephesians 1:18 | 81
    4.23 Ephesians 4:1, 4 | 82
    4.24 Colossians 3:15 | 83
    4.25 Philippians 3:13–14 | 84
    4.26 Summation | 85

5 Luke's Soteriological Use of Call | 89
   5.1 Introduction | 89
   5.2 Luke 5:27–32 | 90
   5.3 Luke 14:7–14 | 93
   5.4 Luke 14:15–24 | 96
      5.4.1 Israel's Misunderstanding of Election | 98
      5.4.2 The Messianic Banquet Has Begun | 102
      5.4.3 Summation | 104
   5.5 Acts 2:39 | 104
   5.6 Acts 15:17 | 105
   5.7 Summation | 106

6 Conclusions | 108
   6.1 Introduction | 108
   6.2 Call in New Testament Soteriology | 108
   6.3 Call and the Soteriologies of Luke and Paul | 110
   6.4 Call and the Christian Life | 114

   Bibliography | *119*

Acknowledgements

THE FIRST ACKNOWLEDGEMENT FOR this book must be to my colleague Rev. Dr. D. Morcom. His humble academic excellence, his warm encouragement, and fine attention to detail were essential for the production of this book.

My thanks also to Rev. Dr. Don McLellan who freely gave of his time to read the manuscript for me and provide valuable input. Rev. Dr. Charles de Jongh also provided crucial advice early in the process.

My appreciation to the Principal, the Council, and faculty of Malyon College who released and encouraged me to undertake this writing.

Thank you also to the Rev. Megan Powell du Toit, Rev. Dr. Graeme Chatfield, and the Board of Directors of the Australian College of Theology for the financial support necessary to get this book to publishing. To Greta Morris, thanks for all of the attention to detail.

The love of my family, Lynette, Olivia, and Brooke, always helped to keep things in perspective. Thanks for bringing joy in hard times.

Finally, thanks to God for not only providing the awe-inspiring Scriptures which this book humbly seeks to explore, but the opportunity to do so. Your grace continues to amaze me.

Abbreviations

OT	Old Testament
Gen	Genesis
Exod	Exodus
Lev	Leviticus
Num	Numbers
Deut	Deuteronomy
Josh	Joshua
Judg	Judges
Ruth	Ruth
1–2 Sam	1–2 Samuel
1–2 Kgs	1–2 Kings
1–2 Chr	1–2 Chronicles
Ezra	Ezra
Neh	Nehemiah
Esth	Esther
Job	Job
Ps/Pss	Psalms
Prov	Proverbs
Eccl	Ecclesiastes
Isa	Isaiah
Jer	Jeremiah
Lam	Lamentations
Ezek	Ezekiel
Dan	Daniel
Hos	Hosea
Joel	Joel
Amos	Amos
Mic	Micah
Zeph	Zephaniah

Zech	Zechariah
Mal	Malachi
NT	New Testament
Matt	Matthew
Mark	Mark
Luke	Luke
John	John
Acts	Acts
Rom	Romans
1–2 Cor	1–2 Corinthians
Gal	Galatians
Eph	Ephesians
Phil	Philippians
Col	Colossians
1–2 Thess	1–2 Thessalonians
1–2 Tim	1–2 Timothy
1–2 Pet	1–2 Peter
Rev	Revelation
LXX	Septuagint
Lit.	Literally
NPP	New Perspective on Paul

I

Introduction

1.1 Called or Invited?

WHEN I WAS STUDYING the New Testament with respect to the process of conversion in the early church, I was struck by the occurrence of καλέω ("call") and its cognates in both the parable of the Great Banquet and Paul's description of the details of conversion in Romans 8. In Luke 14:15–24 the rich man/king "invited" (ἐκάλεσεν) the guests to the great banquet. In Romans 8:28–30 Paul wrote:

> And we know that for those who love God all things work together for good, for those who are called (κλητοῖς) according to his purpose. For those whom he foreknew he also predestined to be conformed to the image of his Son, in order that he might be the firstborn among many brothers. And those whom he predestined he also called (ἐκάλεσεν), and those whom he called (ἐκάλεσεν); he also justified, and those whom he justified he also glorified.[1]

The different translation of καλέω and its cognates as "invite" and "call" in these salvation contexts piqued my interest and opened the broader vista of the issues related to the soteriologies of Luke and Paul, the major contributors to the New Testament.

The congruence of the theologies of Paul and Luke has been a matter of debate. In particular, according to many scholars, the soteriologies of Paul and Luke are divergent. The usage of καλέω language by both Paul and Luke suggested that it may be a common element in their soteriologies. Yet

---

1. All references are from the ESV unless otherwise indicated.

it does not emerge as one of the key soteriological terms in New Testament scholarship.

The topic of this book is, then, "What role does the call (καλέω) of God play in the soteriologies of Paul and Luke?" The book will examine the soteriological use of καλέω and its cognates in the Pauline corpus and Luke–Acts and will draw conclusions and implications from its use.

1.2 The History of Scholarship on This Topic

The question of the comparative use of καλέω in the soteriologies of Paul and Luke fits within the broader scholarship regarding the relationship between Jesus and Paul and their respective theologies. So, in reviewing the contours of the scholarship on this topic, we will move from the broader issues of Jesus and Paul, through the narrower issues related to Luke and Paul, down to the issue of their soteriologies, and then to the use and meaning of the word καλέω itself.

1.2.1 *Jesus and Paul*

Though Paul may have seen Jesus during his earthly ministry, there is no indication of this in his letters.[2] However, according to Acts, Paul encountered Jesus and came in contact with his followers after the crucifixion. On this basis, there has been a traditional assumption that Paul was exposed to the teaching of Jesus through his disciples and that his theology was founded upon those teachings. This assumption is supported by passages such as 1 Corinthians 11:23 where Paul says he passed on what he "received from the Lord."

However, in 1907, Wrede named Paul "the second founder of Christianity."[3] Since then many scholars have argued that the Christianity of Paul is distinct from that of Jesus of Nazareth.[4] Key to this is what Wenham calls the "embarrassing" failure of Paul to make reference to the life or teaching of Jesus.[5] Paul frequently refers to the death and resurrection of Jesus, but says little about his birth, baptism, miracles, parables, or transfiguration.

There is also divergence between the message of Jesus, as presented in the Gospels, and the teaching of Paul. While Jesus focuses more on the kingdom of God, Paul focuses more on the death and resurrection of Christ,

---

2. Fraser, *Jesus and Paul*, 46.
3. Wrede, *Paul*.
4. For a summary see Furnish, "The Jesus-Paul Debate: From Baur to Bultmann."
5. Wenham, *Paul: Follower of Jesus or Founder of Christianity?*, 3.

and justification by faith. Paul is also distinct from Jesus in his interest in the Holy Spirit and the Gentile mission, his negative attitude towards the OT Law, and his teachings on the church as the "body" of Christ.

A subset of this issue is the apparent divergence between the theologies of Luke and Paul, the two major contributors to the New Testament.

1.2.2 Luke and Paul

Luke and Paul have traditionally been associated with one another. The early church's ascription of the authorship of the Third Gospel and Acts to Luke and the use of "we" passages in Acts (for example, Acts 16:11) has been taken to indicate that Luke was a companion of Paul on his travels. However, some of the objections to Lukan authorship of Luke–Acts have been based on the theological differences between Acts and the Pauline Epistles.[6] For example, some point to the way that Paul advocates the circumcision of Timothy in Acts while he opposes it in Galatia. Similarly, Paul's sermons in Acts are said not to reflect the theology of the Pauline Epistles.[7]

While the issue of the authorship of Luke and Acts has some relevance, the focus of this book is the *theology* of the writings traditionally attributed to Luke and Paul. As a result, the issue of authorship will not be examined in depth. However, the apparent theological differences between Luke–Acts and Paul which are used to question Lukan authorship are of great relevance. In arguing that Luke did not write the books traditionally ascribed to him Vielhauer[8] identifies four areas of difference between Luke–Acts and Paul:

1. Natural Theology: There is a contrast between Paul's Areopagus speech in Acts 17 and Romans 1:21.

2. The Law: There is an absence in Acts of the Pauline emphasis on freedom from the law.

3. Christology: Paul's emphasis on the "Cosmic Christ" is missing from Luke–Acts.

4. Eschatology: Faced by the apparent "delay" in the Parousia, Luke develops a history of salvation where the ministry of Jesus fits between the age of the prophets and the age of the church recorded in Acts.[9] Such an eschatology is said to be in sharp contrast with that of Paul.

---

6. Guthrie, *New Testament Introduction*.
7. Haenchen, *The Acts of the Apostles*, 112–6.
8. Quoted in Ellis, *The Gospel of Luke*, 45–50.
9. See Conzelmann, *The Theology of St. Luke*.

Kümmel concludes that the author of the Third Gospel "is obviously a total stranger to the theology of Paul."[10] This is because for the author of the Third Gospel, the death of Jesus is seen as a "transition to heavenly glory in accordance with divine necessity (9:22; 17:25; 24:26)" and the Markan references to Christ's expiatory death (10:45; 15:34) are omitted. Further, Luke has little on justification by faith, highlights Jesus' resurrection rather than his crucifixion, and does not share Paul's imminent eschatology.[11]

While many scholars have critiqued these arguments for the separation of the theologies of Luke and Paul,[12] the question of the apparent differences in the soteriologies of Luke–Acts and the Pauline Epistles remains of considerable importance because of the centrality of salvation to the Christian faith.

1.2.3 The Soteriologies of Luke and Paul

Salvation is a major theme of the Pauline writings. Paul uses the verb σῴζω ("to save") twenty-nine times (which is more than anyone else in the NT), the noun σωτήρ ("savior") twelve times (exactly half its NT occurrences), σωτηρία ("salvation") eighteen times, σωτήριον ("salvation") and σωτήριος ("bringing salvation") once each. He also uses ῥύομαι ("to rescue") eleven times.

Luke also refers to salvation frequently. He uses σωτηρία four times (1:69, 71, 77; 2:30), and σωτήριον twice (3:6; 19:9) in his Gospel. He also uses σωτήρ twice (1:47; 2:11), and employs the verb σῴζω (9:24; 19:10) more often than the other evangelists. Hence, Marshall concludes that the idea of salvation supplies the key to Luke's theology.[13]

However, the soteriologies of Paul and Luke have differences. When Paul uses the term "salvation" (σωτηρία), he means being saved from the eschatological wrath of God with the result that the one who is saved receives eternal life in the form of a resurrected body (Rom 10:1, 10; 11:11; 13:11; 2 Cor 1:6; 6:2; 7:10; Eph 1:13; Phil 1:19, 28; 2:12; 1 Thess 5:8–9; 2 Thess 2:13; 2 Tim 2:10; 3:15). The foundation of Paul's soteriology is the nature of God. Although God is a righteous judge (Rom 1–2), in his relationship with human beings he shows love, grace, and kindness. Paul's denial of the possibility of gaining salvation by the works of the law (Gal 2:16) leads him to advocate a solution to the problem of human sin and its eternal consequences

---

10. Kümmel, *Introduction to the New Testament*, 149.
11. Bird, "Introduction," 5.
12. See Ellis, *The Gospel of Luke*, 42–52.
13. Marshall, *Luke: Historian and Theologian*, 92.

that is completely independent of all human effort. Paul draws on a range of images from different realms to explain how the death and resurrection of Jesus Christ can save people: justification, substitution, redemption, reconciliation, atonement, participation, and sonship (Rom 3:24-26, 30; 4:24-5:1; 5:9, 16-21; cf. 1 Cor 6:11; Gal 2:21; 3:11-14).[14] These metaphors provide a framework for describing and understanding Paul's soteriology.

However, these terms and metaphors used by Paul are largely absent from the soteriology of the Gospels. Indeed, a case can be made that Luke's understanding of Jesus' death is non-soteriological.[15] Luke does not use Mark 10:45 in his Gospel and Jesus' words over the bread and cup (Luke 22:15-19a) do not, in the mind of many scholars, interpret Jesus' death soteriologically, particularly as a vicarious atonement. When Luke quotes from Isaiah 53:12 in Luke 22:37, he omits the final part of the verse, "For he bore the sin of many, and made intercession for the transgressors" which refers to vicarious atonement. After reviewing the scholarship, Talbert can conclude that Luke did not develop a positive doctrine of the redemptive significance of the passion or the cross.[16]

Indeed, there is no consensus concerning what the precise source of salvation is in Luke's soteriology.[17] Suggestions include the resurrection-ascension-exaltation[18] and Jesus' position as the Lord presently reigning in heaven.[19] Larkin argues that a proper understanding of the use of Isaiah 53:12 in Luke 22:37 reveals that the interaction of certain theological themes in the Passion Narrative serve as the objective foundation for understanding the death of Jesus as a vicarious atonement.[20]

However, despite this lack of consensus, several scholars have already attempted to use soteriology to bridge the supposed "gap" between the theologies of Paul and Luke.[21] Borgen[22] identified that both Luke and Paul depend on Deuteronomy 29:4 ("But to this day the LORD has not given you a heart to understand or eyes to see or ears to hear") to interpret the rejec-

14. Powell, *Introducing the New Testament: A Historical, Literary, and Theological Survey*, 263.
15. Franklin, *Christ the Lord: A Study in the Purpose and Theology of Luke–Acts*, 65.
16. Talbert, "Shifting Sands: The Recent Study of the Gospel of Luke," 389.
17. Larkin, "Luke's Use of the Old Testament as a Key to His Soteriology," 323.
18. Martin, "Salvation and Discipleship in Luke's Gospel," 367.
19. Franklin, *Christ the Lord: A Study in the Purpose and Theology of Luke–Acts*, 67.
20. Larkin, "Luke's Use of the Old Testament as a Key to His Soteriology," 327.
21. For this summary, the author is heavily indebted to the work of Morlan, "Conversion in Luke and Paul: Some Exegetical and Theological Explorations."
22. Borgen, "From Paul to Luke: Observations toward Clarification of the Theology of Luke–Acts."

tion of the gospel by Israel (Rom 11:7-8 and Acts 28:26). He also showed that both Paul and Luke see the rejection of Israel as necessary before the gospel could go to the Gentiles (Luke 14:15-24; 20:9-19 and Rom 9-11). Further, both Luke and Paul understand there to be an era "until the time of the Gentiles is fulfilled" (Rom 11:25 and Luke 21:24).

Borgen's approach of choosing a single aspect of theology (e.g. the role of Israel) as a basis for comparison of the soteriology of Luke and Paul has spawned a range of other research utilizing a similar methodology.

Koenig[23] compared Luke and Paul by focusing on their notions of grace. He concluded that there is a deep unity between Luke and Paul in that as both witnessed the expansion of the early church they saw it fundamentally as a work of God's grace in the world.

Jackson[24] highlighted the similarities between Luke's and Paul's pneumatology: (1) the presence of the Holy Spirit shows God's approval, (2) all Christians receive the Spirit at conversion, (3) the fruit of the Spirit's work in the lives of believers, and (4) believers may experience the Spirit in ways that are inseparable from their experience of the Father, Christ, angels, or "the Word."

Killgallen,[25] pointing to the divine conception and other references to the Holy Spirit in Luke-Acts, concluded that for both Paul and Luke, faith, not law, is necessary for the promise of the Holy Spirit to be received.

In contrast, Cho[26] argued that Paul understood the Spirit and the kingdom to be closely associated while Luke did not. For Luke, the Spirit was restricted to certain specific purposes, principally as the power for the proclamation of the kingdom.

In examining the soteriology of Paul and Luke, Lodge[27] concluded the major difference was their contrasting emphasis on eschatology. For Paul, Jesus *will be* the Savior, while for Luke, Jesus *is* Savior at his birth. Paul is concerned with the process of being saved (in 1 Thessalonians each occurrence of salvation terminology (2:16; 5:8, 9) refers to something that has not yet occurred), while Luke stresses the Christ-event that has already saved. Lodge concludes that "the source of our developing Christian awareness of

---

23. Koenig, "Occasions of Grace in Paul, Luke and First Century Judaism."

24. Jackson, "Luke and Paul: A Theology of One Spirit from Two Perspectives."

25. Kilgallen, "A Major Difference between Law and Faith, in Luke and His Traditions."

26. Cho, "Spirit and Kingdom in Luke–Acts: Proclamation as the Primary Role of the Spirit in Relation to the Kingdom of God in Luke–Acts," 197.

27. Lodge, "The Salvation Theologies of Paul and Luke."

the meaning of salvation emerges precisely out of the tension between these two writers."[28]

Taeger[29] conducted a brief survey of how "body" and "flesh" are used in Paul and Luke. While noting a similarity of vocabulary between them, he then suggests Paul's dualism is more sophisticated than Luke's. For Luke, σάρξ was a description of the whole person (Luke 24:39; Acts 2:31), while Paul believed there to be a division between the flesh and spirit (e.g. Rom 7:5, 14, 18, 25; 8:4). It is further suggested that Luke believed humanity, and the terms used by Luke to describe it, are basically neutral—for Luke the problem was not intrinsic to human depravity per se. Taeger concludes that Luke believed humanity did not need to be saved, but just corrected.

Berger[30] argued that Jesus' notion of purity was close to that of the Pharisees yet different enough to upset them. Paul understood his conversion to Jesus to actually fulfill his Pharisaical desire for holiness. In Luke, there is a synthesis of Pharisaical and Gentile notions of purity as they strive to live in unity (Acts 15).

More recently, Porter[31] noted several convergences between the theology of Luke and Paul. He argues that they both:

1. Utilize the OT in a similar manner.

2. Share the perspective that Jesus is "Lord" even if the emphasis may vary.

3. Share the view that Jesus' death was covenantal and expiatory based on a shared knowledge of the Eucharist tradition of 1 Corinthians 11:23–25.

4. Have a compatible understanding of the Parousia.

However, in his doctoral dissertation, Morlan[32] compared conversion in Luke and Paul. He concluded that they differ in their understanding of repentance as well as in the correlation between conversion and creation: for Luke, conversion is the restored *imago Dei* of the original creation, while for Paul it is a fresh act by the God of new creation. However, Luke and Paul agree on the centrality of Christology in their conversion theologies and

---

28. Ibid., 52.

29. Taeger, "Paulus Und Lukas Über Den Menschen."

30. Berger, "Jesus Als Pharisäer Und Frühe Christen Als Pharisäer." As summarised in Morlan, "Conversion in Luke and Paul: Some Exegetical and Theological Explorations," 8.

31. Porter, "Luke: Companion or Disciple of Paul."

32. Morlan, "Conversion in Luke and Paul: Some Exegetical and Theological Explorations."

understand successful conversion to be impossible without the intervention of an agency outside of the pre-convert.

Morlan argues that for Paul, agency in conversion begins with a strong notion of God's calling.[33] Within this notion of divine agency, human agency is explained as a human call and confession to God about Jesus' achievement of resurrection (Rom 10:9–13). In contrast, Luke's *starting point* in describing conversion is not divine agency, but human reasoning and curiosity. The son (Luke 15) comes to his senses first and then comes to the father. Similarly, in Acts 17, the Athenians ask questions, are seeking after God, worshipping him, then later find out what it is God has done with the "man" with whom God will judge the world.

However, as Morlan has acknowledged, his investigation of conversion in Paul and Luke was limited to certain, well chosen, passages.[34] This book aims to build on Morlan's work on the question of conversion in Paul and Luke by turning attention to a single word, καλέω, and its cognates, and examining how that word is used by these two authors in the context of salvation.

1.2.4 The Word καλέω

With reference to its classical usage, Arndt, Danker, and Bauer[35] identify that καλέω can be used in four ways:

1. To identify by name—to name:
   - call (to someone) with naming implied
   - call, address as, designate
   - name, provide with a name

Very often the emphasis is that the bearers of the name actually *are* what the name says about them. The passive, to be named, thus approaches closely the meaning "to be." For example: "So was fulfilled what was said through the prophets, that he would be called a Nazarene" (Matt 2:23).

2. To request the presence of someone at a social gathering—to invite. For example: "'And that's not all,' Haman added. 'I'm the only person Queen Esther invited (κέκληκεν) to accompany the king to the banquet

---

33. Ibid., 229.

34. Ibid., 19–20.

35. Arndt et al., *A Greek-English Lexicon of the New Testament and Other Early Christian Literature*, 502–4.

she gave. And she has invited me along with the king tomorrow'" (Esth 5:12 LXX).

3. To use authority to have a person or group appear—summon
   - call together
   - summon
   - a legal term—call in, summon before a court

For example: "Then they called them in again and commanded them not to speak or teach at all in the name of Jesus" (Acts 4:18). Often there is a hint of privilege and command in the use of καλέω. There is the implication that if a person ignores this invitation they are squandering life and hope.

4. From the meanings "summon" and "invite" there develops the extended sense of choice for receipt of a special benefit or experience. For example, "And no one takes this honor on himself, but he receives it when called by God, just as Aaron was" (Heb 5:4).

Numerous compounds of the simple verb appear in the classical literature.[36] The verb is frequently observed in the Homeric epics where it is used to issue a request or command for someone to be present, or to bestow a name on someone or something.[37] The adjective (κλητός) is also found twice in Homer where "called" clearly implies "chosen." As will be demonstrated later, the writers of the LXX, Luke and Paul, all understood it in this way.

Greek society did not have a sense of work as divine call or vocation.[38] The term was reserved for priests and to some extent to those who devoted themselves to intellectual and administrative tasks. Such a use was more common in the mystery religions (e.g. that of Isis), the LXX and the NT. It is notable, however, that Epictetus rebukes those who complain about their situation because they are disgracing "the calling with which he (God) called them" (τὴν κλῆσιν ἣν κέκληκεν) (*Discourses*, 1.29.49).[39] Such language is echoed in the New Testament.

In the LXX καλέω occurs 480 times, mainly in Genesis as part of the Semitic idiom for giving a name to a person or place. It is prominent in Isaiah, occurring fifty-nine times. When Jewish people are "called" "priests

---

36. Silva, *New International Dictionary of New Testament Theology and Exegesis*, 2, 601–7.

37. Homer, *The Illiad*, Book 2. "I will either forfeit my own head and be no more called father of Telemachus..."

38. Silva, *New International Dictionary of New Testament Theology and Exegesis*, 2, 602.

39. Chester, *Conversion at Corinth*, 72.

of the Lord God" (Isa 61:6) or "sons of the living God" (Hos 1:10), this is equivalent to God giving his servants "another name" (Isa 65:15), which implies a new existence:

> You will leave your name
> for my chosen ones to use in their curses;
> the Sovereign LORD will put you to death,
> but to his servants he will give another name.[40]

The compound ἐπικαλέω is more frequent in theologically significant contexts. For example, Jeremiah 14:9b says "You are among us, LORD, and we bear your name." To bear God's name means to be identified with him and enjoy his intimacy and protection. καλέω often refers to the call issued by someone who is in higher rank than the one who is summoned, for example, parents-children (Gen 24:58), rulers-subjects (Exod 1:18, Judg 12:1), Moses-elders (Exod 12:21; 19:7). However, such a command is not what Silva calls a "despotic compulsion", citing the example of Job 13:22, "Then summon me and I will answer." People sometimes refuse to hear and obey the call of God (Isa 50:2; 65:12; Jer 7:13; 13:10). Yet, at the same time, God's commanding call cannot be frustrated: it creates order in the universe (Isa 40:26) and causes events to happen in history (Ps 105:16; Jer 25:29).[41]

In the later chapters of Isaiah, especially the Servant Songs, καλέω is frequently used with ἐκλέγομαι ("to choose"). It is the elect one (Isa 41:8–9; 43:10) whom God calls in righteousness (42:6), and by name (43:1; 45:3):

> But you, Israel, my servant,
> Jacob, whom I have chosen,
> the offspring of Abraham, my friend;
> you whom I took from the ends of the earth,
> and called from its farthest corners,
> saying to you, "You are my servant,
> I have chosen you and not cast you off" (Isa 41:8–9).

Of the 230 occurrences of καλέω and its compounds in the NT, nearly half are found in Luke–Acts. The verb is used in the divine sense twenty-seven times in the generally accepted letters of Paul, although once (1 Cor 10:27) it refers to an invitation to a meal party.[42] The noun κλῆσις occurs

---

40. NIV translation.

41. Silva, *New International Dictionary of New Testament Theology and Exegesis*, 2, 603.

42. Schmidt, "Καλέω," 487–91.

eleven times in the NT, all but two of them in the Pauline corpus (Heb 3:1 and 2 Pet 1:10). Seven out of the ten occurrences of the adjective κλητός are also Pauline.[43]

In the Gospels, the term is used where God gives a name. Conferring the names of Jesus (Luke 1:31) and John (Luke 1:13) expresses, as in the OT, God's control over their lives.[44] Jesus uses καλέω when he says, "I came not to call the righteous, but sinners" (Matt 9:13; Mark 2:17; Luke 5:32). It is fairly common in Matthew but less so in Mark and John. Luke uses the word nine times in the parable of the Great Banquet (Luke 14:16–25), and Matthew uses it five times in his parable of the marriage feast (Matt 22:2–10). There are rabbinic parables which are reminiscent of Luke 14:16–25 and Matthew 22:2–10 both in general thought and details. The idea of invitation or summoning to the blessings of salvation was familiar to the rabbis.[45] καλέω is also used in Revelation 19:9 of those who are invited to the Lamb's marriage feast. In each case, the invitation was effectively to enter the kingdom of God.

The word καλέω and its cognates have been translated in various ways as will now be examined.

1.2.5 *The Translation of* καλέω

Consciously or unconsciously, systematic theologians have tended to distinguish between the Gospels and the Epistles when it comes to the use of καλέω. They distinguish between a general calling to salvation[46]—an invitation extended to all people (Matt 22:2–14, Luke 14:16–26)—and "the effective call."[47] For example, Grudem, after listing the various usages of "call" in the Epistles concludes, "These verses indicate that no powerless, merely human calling is in view. The calling is like the 'summons' from the king of the universe and as such it brings about the response that it asks for in people's hearts."[48] He goes on to say, "In distinction from effective calling, which is entirely an act of God, we may talk about the *gospel call* in general which comes through human speech. This gospel call is offered to all people,

---

43. Silva, *New International Dictionary of New Testament Theology and Exegesis*, 2, 604.

44. Ibid.

45. See, for example, Babylonian Talmud Shabbath 153a.

46. Erickson, *Christian Theology*, 930.

47. Ryrie, *Basic Theology: A Popular Systemic Guide to Understanding Biblical Truth*, 325.

48. Grudem, *Systematic Theology: An Introduction to Biblical Doctrine*, 692.

even those who do not accept it."⁴⁹ This distinction has created a dichotomy between the so-called "general call" of the Gospels and the "effective call" of the Pauline Epistles.

Whether translators have been influenced by this dichotomy or not, καλέω and its cognates have been translated in different ways in different places. For example, in Luke 14:16 ("A man once gave a great banquet and invited many") ἐκάλεσεν is translated as "invited" by the ESV. However, in 1 Corinthians 1:9 ("God is faithful, by whom you were called into the fellowship of his Son, Jesus Christ our Lord") ἐκλήθητε is translated as "called." It could be argued that the different translations of καλέω as "call" or "invite" are because a host invites but a king calls. However, in Matthew 22 where the banquet is hosted by the king, the guests are still "invited" (κεκλημένους) in most translations.

One must be sympathetic to the problem the translators face in seeking to substitute a word in one language for a word in another language when the original word is being used in different contexts and may have different meanings in those contexts. However, the meanings of the different English words that are used to translate καλέω and its cognates are quite different. For instance, the English word "call" has a broad range of meanings including:⁵⁰

- to speak in a loud distinct voice so as to be heard at a distance
- to make a request or demand
- of an animal: to utter a characteristic note or cry
- to utter in a loud distinct voice
- to announce or read loudly or authoritatively
- to command or request to come or be present
- to cause to come
- to summon to a particular activity
- to invite or command to meet

In contrast "invite" means:⁵¹

- to offer an incentive or inducement to
- to increase the likelihood of

---

49. Ibid., 693.
50. Merriam-Webster Dictionary, "Call."
51. "Invite."

- to request the presence or participation of
- to request formally
- to urge politely

Although invitation can be thought of as a subset of the meaning of call, the latter term is much broader in meaning and carries stronger undertones of authority. If these two different English words are used to translate the same Greek word καλέω, it must be done so carefully and in light of the context of the word in the text, not theological predispositions.

If the predestination debate can be set aside, a more sensitive examination of the use of καλέω in the NT may be undertaken. For example, Berkhof also distinguished between external and internal call, but conceded, "While we distinguish two aspects of the calling of God, this calling is really one. The internal call is really the external call made effective by the operation of the Holy Spirit."[52] This approach foreshadows a more deductive (as opposed to inductive) approach to examining the call of God by Luke and Paul as proposed in this research.

1.3 What You Need to Know About This Book

The overall aim of this book is to examine the role of καλέω and its cognates in the soteriologies of Luke and Paul and to draw conclusions and implications from its use. Hence, the focus will be the soteriological use of καλέω in the NT writings of Luke–Acts and the Epistles of Paul.

The study will be limited to Luke–Acts rather than all of the Gospels because of the prevalence of καλέω in this gospel and the need to keep the scope of the volume to a manageable size. Further, the focus on Luke–Acts means the findings will also be able to feed directly into the Luke–Paul debate.

The focus will be on the traditionally accepted Pauline corpus with the exception of the Pastoral Epistles. Many scholars accept that even if Paul did not write Colossians, Ephesians, and 2 Thessalonians they reflect his theological position. For example, Martin concludes that Ephesians was written by "a well-known disciple and companion of Paul who published this letter under the apostle's aegis either during the apostle's final imprisonment or (more probably) after his death."[53] This position is less widely accepted with respect to the Pastoral Epistles. Further, even though the author does use

---

52. Berkhof, *Systematic Theology*, Chapter 19.
53. Martin, *Ephesians, Colossians and Philemon*, 4.

call language soteriologically in the Pastoral Epistles (1 Tim 6:12; 2 Tim 1:9), to omit these texts from the analysis does not undermine the conclusions we will reach.

Paul speaks not only of the call of God to humanity, but also the human response of calling on the name of the Lord (Rom 10:13). Although this response is clearly part of the process of salvation, it does represent a different, but related, concept. Hence, this usage will not be analyzed here, although it will play a part in the discussion of the soteriology of Paul. The specific passages that will be the focus of this research will be those where Paul and Luke speak of the call of God to humans or humanity.

The approach will be one of biblical theology rather than systematic theology. Biblical theology is here defined as an approach that seeks to systematize the teaching of the Bible in contrast to systematic theology which consciously attempts to express the truth of God in ways relevant to and understandable by contemporary culture.[54] In maintaining this distinction, this book will look for lines of connection and emphasis that are natural to the biblical material itself rather than imposed upon it from traditional dogmatics.[55]

The book will also be more "theological" than "exegetical." Exegesis is important but by itself can be overly analytical and atomistic.[56] Biblical theology causes the reader to more seriously consider the text in the light of the entire unit, book, and the Bible as a whole. However, that does not mean that an apparently idiosyncratic text cannot stand in its own right even if it means refining and adjusting the previous understanding.

While acknowledging the benefits of exegetical study, the field of semantics brings some important provisos to its use. In some models of exegesis, the assumption is that words are the basic carriers of meaning, whilst sentences convey the exact sum of the semantic values of their verbal components.[57] Hence, the technique is to move over a text "word by word," atomizing language into ever-smaller and smaller units. However, in this book, atomizing exegesis which pays insufficient attention to context will be avoided.

Another error to be avoided is the assumption that the etymological meaning of a word is somehow its "basic" or "proper" meaning.[58] It can be

---

54. Fanning, "Theological Analysis," 284.

55. Ibid., 280.

56. Osborne, *The Hermeneutical Spiral: A Comprehensive Introduction to Biblical Interpretation*, 82.

57. Thiselton, "Semantics and New Testament Interpretation," 78.

58. Ibid., 80.

misleading to base the meanings of words on their use in classical Greek or their etymologies. In addition, James Barr[59] has criticized many of the articles in Kittel's *Theological Dictionary of the New Testament*, based on what he calls "illegitimate totality transfer." This is where the semantic value of a word as it occurs in one context is added to its semantic value in another context; and the process is continued until the sum of these semantic values is then read into a particular case. However, this approach denies the reality that words are arbitrary symbols that carry meaning only in contexts, and will be avoided.

Another semantic insight which will be used here is the idea that "meaning is choice." Halliday[60] argues that choice, as the core mechanism for expressing meaning, creates a contrast between what is chosen and what is not, but could have been. Choice is how meaning is created. Interpreters cannot fully understand the author's use of a word until they also know what alternatives were available to the author at the same time.

Hence, the biblical analysis will take the two-stage approach identified by Fanning.[61] In the analytical stage, textual criticism, background studies, grammar, flow of argument, lexical studies, use of the OT, and genre considerations will be utilized. In the synthetic stage, the goal is to construct biblical theology based upon the analytical stage. This approach does not look at words in isolation but at propositions and paragraphs using these words and the theological ideas expressed in them.

Careful grammatical, exegetical, and concept-oriented terminological analysis of the texts under examination will provide the foundation for the theological observations. The OT and socio-historical background will especially inform understanding.

Paul's theology is more easily derived because his epistolary medium allowed him to be more explicit in his language. However, because Luke is using narrative to convey his theology,[62] conclusions must be derived more cautiously. Still, a single story can be considered a significant text. Themes that recur in the Lukan narratives give scholars more confidence in determining important aspects of Luke's theology, but each narrative is important in its own right.

In the case of the gospel passages, historical-critical methods will be used as appropriate. I will utilize redaction criticism with a view to

---

59. Barr, *The Semantics of Biblical Language*, 218.

60. Halliday, *Language as Social Semiotic: The Social Interpretation of Language and Meaning*, 3–6.

61. Fanning, "Theological Analysis," 287.

62. Green, *The Theology of the Gospel of Luke*, 3.

discovering the distinctive features of Luke's theology with respect to καλέω. Redaction criticism can give insight into the theological motives that shape Luke's handling of his material. However, while the alterations made by Luke are important evidence of his theology, the theology itself is to be extracted from the texts as a whole, rather than *just* the redactions.

A key passage is the parable of the Great Banquet (Luke 14). The interpretation of parables requires careful attention. Bailey[63] has pointed out that a proper hermeneutical methodology for the parables must take into account the nature and purpose of the parables as both a particular genre of literature and the reasons Jesus employed them. The intended appeal for ancient readers provides the framework for proper interpretation. From the historical (the original setting), literary (gospel setting), and cultural contexts, the structure and details of the parabolic narratives may be studied to derive the central message of the parables, which usually have as their referent some specific aspect of God's kingdom program.

These guidelines will mean that while it may be overambitious to claim to understand Luke and Paul's thoughts behind the use of καλέω, we will have been led to conclusions, to some extent, by Luke and Paul themselves.

1.4 Why This Book Is Important

The writings of Luke and Paul form a significant portion of the NT and as a result they make a major contribution to Christian theology. This book builds upon the work of other scholars who have compared and contrasted theological usage of certain terms by both Paul and Luke. Although others have examined the concept of conversion in Luke and Paul, a detailed examination of the use of the word καλέω and its cognates represents a significant lacuna in the existing scholarship. This book will not only build understanding of conversion but also of the broader doctrine of soteriology.

Paul uses a variety of metaphors to describe salvation (see chapter 3). On the whole, Protestant scholarship has focused on the judicial metaphors related to δικαιοσύνη (justification/righteousness). This has led some to conclude that Luke has little to say about the means of salvation because he does not use the categories identified by Paul. This book will highlight Luke's use of a metaphor of salvation which Paul also uses. It will be shown that they both use καλέω soteriologically. This not only confirms it as an important metaphor but also addresses accusations that Luke lacks a developed soteriology.

---

63. Bailey, "Guidelines for Interpreting Jesus' Parables."

Most commentaries make passing reference to καλέω as a soteriological concept. However, it does not share the same status as other soteriological concepts such as adoption, justification, or redemption. In a recent volume on salvation in the NT,[64] 522 pages were dedicated to an analysis of the soteriology in the NT. The volume did not contain an index, but a scan through the chapters dedicated to Luke and Paul appeared to indicate that not one section was dedicated to call. Indeed, there appeared to be only three sentences dedicated to the topic in the whole volume.[65] One must be sympathetic to the challenge of attempting to address the topic as vast as soteriology in one volume. However, the scant reference to καλέω in this volume and in others reflects its humble position in the strata of concepts related to salvation.

Since this book will show that καλέω can be identified as present in the soteriology of both Luke and Paul, a case can be made for taking it more seriously as a soteriological concept. The investigation of the καλέω broadens and deepens our understanding of salvation through the elevation of a different category. In particular, the concept of call provides a powerful connection to the OT categories of salvation, as will be demonstrated. As such, it contributes towards a more holistic and satisfying conception of salvation.[66]

If καλέω is recognized as a soteriological term of greater importance than has previously been recognized, then there are also implications for Christian self-identity and behavior. Each metaphor of salvation sheds light on the Christian life and each should be carefully considered and applied. An increased appreciation of καλέω will bring with it implications for Christian life and practice.

The book also sheds light on the most helpful English translation of καλέω and its cognates. Our understanding of the activity of God and the nature of his people's response is nuanced by the translation. The difference between the English words "invite" and "call" is subtle, but important. It is hoped that this work will clarify the soteriological use of καλέω for others and so shed light on its translation.

---

64. van der Watt, *Salvation in the New Testament: Perspectives on Soteriology.*

65. de Villiers, "Soteriological Perspectives in 1 Thessalonians," 314.

66. For more on this see Hussey, "The Soteriological Use of 'Call' in the New Testament: An Undervalued Category?."

1.5 The Structure of This Book

The goal of this book is to discuss Luke's and Paul's understanding and usage of καλέω without imposing modern categories on the ancient writers. Crucial to this is identifying what Luke, Paul, and their readers would have understood by the use of the word καλέω and its cognates. What is to be avoided is the practice of implying a meaning for a word based on a preexisting dogma.

The structure of this book is as follows. Chapter 2 will form the foundation from which the detailed examination of Paul and Luke's use of καλέω can be based. Their use of the word was based on an understanding informed by the technical use of the concept of call in the Old Testament, but also a range of related concepts including election, the covenants, the covenant meal, and the expectation of the eschatological banquet.

The second layer of foundation necessary to interpret their usage of καλέω is composed of Paul and Luke's distinct soteriologies which are surveyed in chapter 3. An analysis of the soteriological usage of καλέω by Paul and Luke will then be performed separately in chapters 4 and 5. From this analysis, comparisons and contrasts in the use of καλέω by Paul and Luke will be identified in the final chapter. Implications will be identified and discussed.

2

Old Testament Background

2.1 Introduction

THE MEANING JESUS, LUKE, and Paul attached to a word like καλέω would have been strongly influenced by their Second Temple Jewish context. Although Luke was a Gentile, there is ample evidence in Luke–Acts of his extensive awareness of the OT, and, debatably, the tutorage of Jewish Christ-followers such as Paul.

This chapter will demonstrate that while one of the central themes in the OT is the covenant relationship between YHWH and "his people," one of the concepts associated with the covenants is the notion of their unilateral election by YHWH. Also associated with covenants in the first-century Jewish mind were the concepts of "naming" and covenant meals. Associated with the covenant meal in Second Temple Judaism was the expectation of a great messianic banquet at the consummation of the age. In order to begin to understand what Luke and Paul intended by their selection of the word καλέω in their writings, we must understand these other related terms because they form the foundational background for interpretation.

2.2 The Call of Israel

In the LXX καλέω is used for the Hebrew word *qārā*. In the OT *qārā* means:[1]

1. To call someone, call someone over: For example, Genesis 12:18: "So Pharaoh called Abram and said . . ."

---

1. Koehler et al., *The Hebrew and Aramaic Lexicon of the Old Testament*, 1128.

2. To call, shout: For example, Genesis 39:14: Potiphar's wife "called to the men of her household and said to them . . ."

3. To name a name for, give someone a name: For example, Ruth 4:17: "And the women of the neighborhood gave him a name, saying, 'A son has been born to Naomi.' They named him Obed."

4. To appoint: For example, Isaiah 49:1: "The LORD called me from the womb, from the body of my mother he named my name."

5. To call, summon:

   a. To the instigation or conduct of legal proceedings: For example, Deuteronomy 25:8, "Then the elders of his city shall call him and speak to him."

   b. To conscript, muster (military service): For example, Judges 8:1: "Then the men of Ephraim said to him, 'What is this that you have done to us, not to call us when you went to fight against Midian?'"

   c. To summon, invite to eat: For example, Genesis 31:54: "Jacob offered a sacrifice in the hill country and called his kinsmen to eat bread." (Used with respect to a sacrificial meal in Exod 34:15, Num 25:2, Deut 33:19, 1 Sam 9:13, 16:3.)

qārā is also used in Genesis 2:20: "The man gave names to all livestock and to the birds of the heavens and to every beast of the field." In the ancient world, to give a person a name was also a sign of authority over him or her (for example, 2 Kgs 23:34; "And Pharaoh Neco made Eliakim the son of Josiah king in the place of Josiah his father, and changed his name to Jehoiakim"). To proclaim the name over something was also a legal act by which ownership was claimed and established.[2] So Adam's naming of the animals was the designation of his dominion over them.[3]

The first person to receive a direct call from God was Abram (Gen 12:1–9).[4] Abram's election was an unconditioned expression of the divine free will. Although his righteousness is subsequently identified, Abram is not distinguished from his peers prior to his election.[5] Calvin concluded, "This calling of Abram is a signal instance of the gratuitous mercy of God. Had Abram been beforehand with God by any merit of works? Had Abram come

---

2. Christensen, *Deuteronomy 21:10–34:12*, 6b, 673.
3. Ellison, "Genesis 1–11," 117.
4. Ryken et al., *Dictionary of Biblical Imagery*, 133.
5. Eslinger, "Prehistory in the Call to Abraham," 194.

to him, or conciliated his favor? Nay, we must ever recall to mind . . . that he was plunged in the filth of idolatry."⁶

In Genesis 17, YHWH "names" Abram:

> No longer will you be called (*yiqqārê*; LXX: κληθήσεται) Abram; your name will be Abraham, for I have made you a father of many nations. I will make you very fruitful; I will make nations of you, and kings will come from you. I will establish my covenant as an everlasting covenant between me and you and your descendants after you for the generations to come, to be your God and the God of your descendants after you (Gen 17:5-7).

When YHWH changed Abram's name to Abraham and Sarai's name to Sarah it signified both a reiteration of the covenant promise and the designation of these people as his chosen servants.⁷

The content of the calling was specifically to "go from your country and your kindred and your father's house to the land that I will show you" (Gen 12:1), but it was in essence a call to life of relationship with him. This relationship with YHWH is salvific as suggested by numerous OT passages like Psalm 86:2: "Reserve my life, for I am godly; save your servant, who trusts in you—you are my God." And so, the link between call and salvation is established through relationship and trust.

The author of the Epistle to the Hebrews recognized that Abram's call was salvific in nature. In 11:8 he/she says: "By faith Abraham obeyed when he was called to go out to a place that he was to receive as an inheritance." Such faith was identified as winning God's approval (Heb 11:2, 6).

Subsequently, the general call of God is extended to the nation of Israel in Deuteronomy 28:9-10:

> The Lord will establish you as a people holy to himself, as he has sworn to you, if you keep the commandments of the Lord your God and walk in his ways. And all the peoples of the earth shall see that you are called (*niqrā*, LXX: ἐπικαλέω) by the name of the Lord, and they shall be afraid of you.

Similarly, in Isaiah 43:1:

> But now thus says the Lord,
> he who created you, O Jacob,
> he who formed you, O Israel:
> Fear not, for I have redeemed you;
> I have called (*qārāṯî*, LXX: ἐκάλεσά) you by name, you are mine.

---

6. Calvin, "Comment to Genesis 12:1."

7. Matthews et al., "Genesis 17:3-8."

The link between "caller" and "creator" is apparent. Because YHWH created Israel he owns her, so has the right to "call" her. Israel owes her origin, character, and reason for existence to YHWH. Hence, the people of Israel are the property of God, and so they need not fear their enemies. Being called by YHWH's name (cf. 2 Chr 7:14; Jer 14:9; 15:16; Amos 9:12) is like a badge of his ownership identifying them as his. This is in contrast to all the other nations (Isa 63:19): "We are yours from of old; but you have not ruled over them, they have not been called by your name."

The subsequent use of *qārā* in the relationship between YHWH and his people reflects this notion of dominion and salvation through relationship. This sense would have informed the use of καλέω by Luke and Paul.

2.3 Call and Election

Related to Israel's sense of call was her election. The OT word translated as elected or chosen is the Hebrew *bāḥăr*. It means:[8]

1. Choose, select, desire, prefer, i.e., make a selection between two or more options (Gen 6:2: "And they took as their wives any they chose");

2. Choose, select, desire, prefer, i.e., choose for the purpose of showing special concern for (Deut 7:6: "The LORD your God has chosen you to be a people for his treasured possession");

3. Test try, probe, examine, assay, i.e., to try and learn the genuineness of an object by examination, and observing reaction to a standard (Isa 48:10: "Behold, I have refined you, but not as silver; I have tried you (*beḥartîḵā*) in the furnace of affliction");

4. Choice, best, pertaining to what is the best of a kind or class, implying desirability and acceptance of the object (Prov 8:10: "Take my instruction instead of silver, and knowledge rather than choice gold").

Election finds explicit expression in many places in the OT and is presumed in many others. The verb occurs 164 times in the OT. In ninety-two of these instances the subject is God, and in thirteen instances of the passive the election is by God. Klein goes as far as to say, "Old Testament theology stands firmly on the bedrock of God's election of Israel."[9]

---

8. Swanson, *Dictionary of Biblical Languages with Semantic Domains: Hebrew (Old Testament)*.

9. Klein, *The New Chosen People: A Corporate View of Election*, 25.

YHWH chooses individuals,[10] but also does so corporately.[11] His choice of individuals is less common. Abraham (Neh 9:7), Jacob (Ps 135:4; Mal 1:2), Moses (Num 16:5, 7), David (1 Sam 13:13–14), and the prophets are the objects of God's election. The dominant use of election terminology applies to the nation of Israel. In the Semitic world, unity was prior to diversity and the community prior to the individual.[12] Election is largely a social concept and so it is only rarely that we see election associated with an individual, such as a prophet, and then only for a special task. A typical example of the corporate expression of election is Deuteronomy 7:6: "For you are a people holy to the LORD your God. The LORD your God has chosen you to be a people for his treasured possession, out of all the peoples who are on the face of the earth."

Related to the concept of election is that of "knowing" (*yāḏă*ʿ). This is illustrated in Jeremiah 1:5:

> Before I formed you in the womb I knew you,
> and before you were born I consecrated you;
> appointed you a prophet to the nations.

As God chooses, so he also "knows" the prophet whom he appoints to the task. As he "chose" Israel he also "knows" the nation as a people: "You only have I known of all the families of the earth" (Amos 3:2). Hence, election is also a strongly relational concept.

Normally *bāḥăr* (elect) is translated ἐκλέγομαι (choose) in the LXX. However, seven times it is translated as κλῆσις ("called").[13] As mentioned in chapter 1, the adjective (κλητός) is also found twice in Homer where "called" clearly implies "chosen."[14] This suggests a close relationship between these two terms. The parallelism of Isaiah 41:9 also demonstrates the relationship between "called" and "chosen":

> You whom I took from the ends of the earth,
> and called (LXX: ἐκάλεσά) from its farthest corners,
> saying to you, "You are my servant,
> I have chosen (LXX: ἐξελεξάμην) you and not cast you off.

---

10. Deuteronomy 17:15; 1 Samuel 2:28; 10:24; 16:8, 9, 10; 2 Samuel 6:21; 1 Kings 8:16; 11:34; 14:21; 1 Chronicles 28:4, 5, 6, 10; 29:1; 2 Chronicles 6:5, 6; Nehemiah 9:7; Psalms 65:4; 78:70; 89:3; 105:26; 106:23; Haggai 2:23.

11. Including Deuteronomy 4:37–38; 7:6, 7; 10:15; 14:2; 18:5; 21:5; 1 Kings 3:8; 1 Chronicles 15:2; Psalm 33:12; Isaiah 14:1; Jeremiah 33:24; Ezekiel 20:5; Zechariah 1:17.

12. Shedd, *Man in Community*, 3–41.

13. Quell, "Ἐκλέγομαι," 145.

14. Silva, *New International Dictionary of New Testament Theology and Exegesis*, 2, 601–7.

By the time of the NT this understanding of "election" and the term "call" had become virtually synonymous as evidenced by their use in 2 Peter 1:10: "Therefore, brothers, be all the more diligent to confirm your calling and election (τὴν κλῆσιν καὶ ἐκλογήν) for if you practice these qualities you will never fall." The author of 2 Peter has a predilection for placing two nearly synonymous pairs of words together as he does here.[15] The calling is based on the choice, but by the first century there is probably no great distinction between the two terms. Similarly, in Revelation 17:14, the two words appear to be used synonymously: κλητοί καὶ ἐκλεκτοί καὶ πιστοί ("called and chosen and faithful").

Ironically, one of the central purposes of election is to benefit the non-elect.[16] This is very clear in the election of the patriarchs. God tells Abram, "Through you all the families of the earth shall be blessed" (Gen 12:2–3; 18:18; 22:18). He repeats the commission in his selection of Isaac (Gen 26:4) and Jacob (Gen 28:14).

The descendants of the patriarchs, Israel, are also chosen for the benefit of all the peoples:

> Keep them and do them, for that will be your wisdom and your understanding in the sight of the peoples, who, when they hear all these statutes, will say, "Surely this great nation is a wise and understanding people." For what great nation is there that has a god so near to it as the LORD our God is to us, whenever we call upon him? And what great nation is there, that has statutes and rules so righteous as all this law that I set before you today? (Deut 4:6–8).

Here the purpose of the law is to make Israel ethically and spiritually unique among all the nations and thereby draw other nations to YHWH. This is also reflected in the Mosaic law which provides benefits for foreigners living in Israel (e.g. Lev 23:22; Deut 10:17–19). The prophets also envision Israel as drawing all nations to worship the Lord:[17]

> and many peoples shall come, and say:
> "Come, let us go up to the mountain of the LORD,
> to the house of the God of Jacob,
> that he may teach us his ways
> and that we may walk in his paths."
> For out of Zion shall go the law,
> and the word of the LORD from Jerusalem" (Isa 2:3).

---

15. Bauckham, *2 Peter, Jude*, 50, 190.
16. Colijn, *Images of Salvation in the New Testament*, 233–6.
17. See also Jeremiah 3:17; Micah 4:2; Zechariah 8:22.

Hence, election and its associated concept of call have a missional element. However, καλέω was not only associated with election in Second Temple Judaism. As we have seen, it also has connections with covenant. So now we must examine the understanding of the OT covenant that Luke, Paul, and their Jewish readers shared.

2.4 Call and Covenant

Walther Eichrodt placed covenant at the center of his Old Testament Theology.[18] However, such a bold assertion is not without its opponents. Critics point to the fact that covenant does not have a single meaning and there are portions of the OT which make no reference to it. Yet, the theological significance of covenant cannot be determined merely by etymology and word counts. Word meanings are dependent on context and the importance of a concept cannot be determined by the number of times a particular word appears in a passage. And so, even though the word $b^e r\hat{\imath}\underline{t}$ (covenant) does not appear especially frequently in the OT, its importance is revealed by the centrality of the concept and the allusions to covenant which permeate the OT.

OT covenants typically begin with God's declaration, "I will establish my covenant . . ." (Gen 6:18; Exod 6:4–5). In this sense, the OT God-human covenants are one-sided and reflect the unconditional character of election. The Hebrew word $b^e r\hat{\imath}\underline{t}$ has the root meaning of "bond" or "fetter."[19] The Hebrew idiom for establishing a covenant is "to cut a covenant" because a covenant is made by a sacrifice (Gen 15:7–21; Ps 50:5).[20]

In Exodus 24:9–11, the rite of the covenant-forming is described: a sacrifice was made, the blood of the sacrificial animals was divided in two parts, one of which was poured out against the altar. The stipulations were then read, followed by the response of the people. The remaining blood was then thrown upon the people sealing the oath. Finally, there was a covenant meal:

> Then Moses and Aaron, Nadab, and Abihu, and seventy of the elders of Israel went up, and they saw the God of Israel. There was under his feet as it were a pavement of sapphire stone, like the very heaven for clearness. And he did not lay his hand on the chief men of the people of Israel; they beheld God, and ate and drank.

---

18. Eichrodt, *Theology of the Old Testament*, 1.
19. Anderson and Bishop, *The Contours of Old Testament Theology*, 75.
20. Lillback, "Covenant."

YHWH's covenants include the offspring of the person or people with whom he makes the covenant. This is true in the cases of Adam (Gen 1:27–28; 3:15; Hos 6:7; Rom 5:12–18; 1 Cor 15:22), Noah (Gen 6:18; 9:9), Abraham (Gen 17:7), Moses (Exod 20:4–6, 8–12; 31:16), Aaron (Lev 24:8–9), Phinehas (Num 25:13), David (2 Chr 13:5; 21:7; Jer 33:19–22), and the people of the new covenant (Isa 59:21). This eternal and corporate nature of covenants is crucial to the interpretation of the covenants in the NT.

The essence of YHWH's covenants is captured in the summary promise, "I will be your God, and you shall be my people." For example, to Abraham:

> And I will establish my covenant between me and you and your offspring after you throughout their generations for an everlasting covenant, to be God to you and to your offspring after you. And I will give to you and to your offspring after you the land of your sojournings, all the land of Canaan, for an everlasting possession, and I will be their God (Gen 17:7–8).

The same formula is repeated to Israel:

> I will take you to be my people, and I will be your God, and you shall know that I am the Lord your God, who has brought you out from under the burdens of the Egyptians (Exod 6:7–8).

And then again to King David:

> Moreover, the Lord declares to you that the Lord will make you a house. When your days are fulfilled and you lie down with your fathers, I will raise up your offspring after you, who shall come from your body, and I will establish his kingdom. He shall build a house for my name, and I will establish the throne of his kingdom forever. I will be to him a father, and he shall be to me a son (2 Sam 7:11–14).

The covenant relation of God with Israel as a nation is the chief form in which humanity's sonship and God's fatherhood appear in the OT.[21] Therefore YHWH can say, "Israel is my firstborn son" (Exod 4:22). Later, Hosea can say, "When Israel was a child, I loved him, and out of Egypt I called my son" (Hos 11:1).

The filial relation of Israel to God is summed up and symbolized in a special way in the Davidic king: "I will be his father, and he shall be my son" (2 Sam 7:14 = 1 Chr 17:13). Although not explicit, a number of verses imply YHWH's marriage relationship with Israel as a nation implies individual

---

21. Rees, "Children of God."

Israelites are his children (Hos 2:19, 20; Jer 3:14, 22; Isa 50:1; Ezek 16:20, 21; 23:37).

The "I will be your God, and you shall be my people" motif highlights the overlapping nature of the covenants. Exodus, although describing the forming of a new covenant, still emphasizes the importance of the Abrahamic covenant. With the breaking of the Sinai covenant (Exod 32), the author demonstrates that the patriarchal covenant was still in force (Exod 33:1):

> The LORD said to Moses, "Depart; go up from here, you and the people whom you have brought up out of the land of Egypt, to the land of which I swore to Abraham, Isaac, and Jacob, saying, 'To your offspring I will give it.'"

The Sinai covenant did not replace the patriarchal covenant, but coexisted with it. Similarly, the Davidic covenant should be thought of as the development of the Abrahamic and Mosaic covenants in the context of the monarchy. The Israelite king, although moderated by the priests and prophets, was now the mediator between the Lord and his people. A covenant with the king thus became necessary. This interrelated and simultaneous nature of the covenants meant that in the NT the writers could refer to "the covenants" as an overarching term.

God's election of the people of Israel and the instigation of the covenant are independent of Israel's faithfulness to keeping the terms of her election and covenant. This explains why God can cast away Israel and judge unfaithfulness while recognizing the faithful remnant which does please him and will attain salvation (Isa 65:8–10).

Further, the OT also holds out the hope of a new covenant which will be granted by God to his people (Isa 55:3; 59:21; 61:8; Jer 31:31–40; 32:40; 50:5; Ezek 20:37; 34:25; 37:26; Hos 2:18). Closely associated with the new covenant is the reign of the Messiah (Isa 42:6; 49:8; Mal 3:1) and regeneration through the Holy Spirit (Isa 59:21; Ezek 36:24–38; Joel 2:28–29.)[22]

Overt connections between covenant and call in the OT are rare. In Genesis 17:19, God says, "No, but Sarah your wife shall bear you a son, and you shall call his name Isaac. I will establish my covenant with him as an everlasting covenant for his offspring after him." Earlier, God had promised that he would confirm his eternal covenant with Abraham and his descendants (17:7). Now this promise is focused on the as-yet-unborn Isaac.[23] By telling Sarah that she shall "name" him Isaac, God exercises his covenantal right of authority.

---

22. Ferguson and Packer, *New Dictionary of Theology*, 173–4.
23. Wenham, *Genesis 16–50*, 2, 27.

In Isaiah 42:6 the prophet makes the connection, although in missionary terms:

> I am the Lord; I have called you in righteousness;
> I will take you by the hand and keep you;
> I will give you as a covenant for the people,
> a light for the nations.

The passage does not make it clear who is being addressed, and more than one possibility is open. For example, some interpreters think Cyrus is in view. Most probably, however, we should see the paragraph as linked with verses 1–4, and so addressed to the exiles, and especially to the leaders among them. The exiles longed for their own release; but the purpose for which God has called and will keep them is to provide light for the Gentiles.[24] The exact meaning of the phrase "a covenant for the people" (literally, "a covenant of people") is obscure, and has been much debated. However, the parallelism suggests that Israel is destined to bring to all nations the possibility of a covenant relationship with YHWH. The covenant reference may be to the new covenant, the special blessings of which were later spelled out in Jeremiah 31:31–34. If it is, it may be viewed as confirming the Abrahamic covenant, for this also spoke of blessing for the nations (cf. Gen 12:1–3).[25]

The relationship between the call and covenant is also alluded to in the lament of 63:19:

> We have become like those over whom you have never ruled,
> like those who are not called by your name.

YHWH's lordship of the people was tied up with his covenant relationship with them. His rule of the people here is in parallel with his naming of them.

In Isaiah 66:4, the relationship is also alluded to in reference to Israel's disobedience: "Because I called them, and they did not obey me, I spoke and they did not hear." Although not explicit, the implication is that the disobedience relates to the covenant stipulations. In other instances of Israel failing to respond, similar vocabulary is used.

The relationship between call and covenant is also implied in the naming process. When God established his covenant with Abraham he called him by a different name. Hosea's statement, "When Israel was a child, I loved him, and out of Egypt I called my son" (Hos 11:1), also reflects this association.

24. Payne, "Isaiah," 749.
25. Grogan, "Isaiah," 255.

Certainly, the relationship between call and covenant in the OT is not as clear as the relationship between call and election. However, there *are* connections, as described above. Further, there is a strong connection through the concept of election: YHWH elected Abraham, Israel, and David to form a covenant with them, and call language forms a prominent part of the election concept.

Associated with the concept of covenant in both the ancient Near East and the Bible is the covenant meal. This ritual will now be discussed.

2.5 The Covenant Meal

People in the ancient Near East customarily ate two meals each day: a light midday lunch and the main meal in the evening after work.[26] The main evening meal was an important event where people displayed kinship and friendship. The meals demonstrated honor, social rank in the family, and community, belonging and purity. Social status and role were acted out in the differentiated tasks and expectations around the meals, and the maintenance of balance and harmony at meals was crucial to the sense of overall well-being. The meal was a joyful time, and joyfulness and cheer could be symbolized in a meal (Prov 15:15). For God's chosen people, meals were ways of experiencing and enjoying God's presence and provision.

But the meal time was also a place where Jews "drew the line" between insiders and outsiders in their families, communities, and ethnic group. Jubilees 22:15–17 says: "Keep yourself separate from the nations and do not eat with them . . ."

> Gentiles and strangers either were excluded or had to undergo special ritual cleansing in order to participate in even ordinary meals. There were strict limitations on food, its preparation and its consumption, distinguishing between the ritually clean and the unclean. Concern for holiness, which gave rise to the kosher (*kashrut*) laws of later Judaism, reflect the Jewish conviction that God is present at meals. To eat defiled food or to eat with an "unclean" person would be inappropriate and dishonoring to God.[27]

Covenants were traditionally sealed with a meal. In 1927, William Robertson Smith in his "Lectures on the Religion of the Semites," argued that ideas such as sacrifice, taboo, tithes, and covenant had developed out of

---

26. Ryken et al., *Dictionary of Biblical Imagery*, 544.
27. Ibid., 545.

primitive Semitic communal feasts.[28] He based his arguments on evidence drawn from classical sources, the OT, and comparative anthropology. Smith argued that "the fundamental conception of ancient religion is the solidarity of the gods and their worshippers as part of one organic society."[29] The gods quite literally belonged to the same tribe as the worshippers, and their community was manifested and enacted through the communal meal.

An essential part of the sacred communal meal was consumption of the flesh of the sacrificed animal. In the ancient Semitic communities meat was rarely eaten, and so the sacred communal meals took on a special significance. Animal sacrifice as an offering that achieved atonement only developed with later ideas of guilt or obligation. The original Semitic sacrifices were occasions of joy and revelry for the tribal community in the presence of their gods.[30]

In time, it came to be understood that those who eat and drink together become bound to one another by friendship and mutual obligation. "If the consumption of meat creates a community between the gods and men, it also does so between men."[31] The biblical texts that portray the sealing of a covenant by a communal act of eating and drinking bear the imprint of this primitive Semitic idea.

In Exodus 24, where the contracting of a covenant between the Lord and the Israelites is described, the slaughtering of oxen is mentioned along with the sacrifice and the covenant meal:

> Then Moses and Aaron, Nadab, and Abihu, and seventy of the elders of Israel went up, and they saw the God of Israel. There was under his feet as it were a pavement of sapphire stone, like the very heaven for clearness. And he did not lay his hand on the chief men of the people of Israel; they beheld God, and ate and drank (Exod 24:9–11).

When Laban and Jacob made a covenant (binding agreement) of peace with each other at Mizpah they ate a meal together: "He offered a sacrifice there in the hill country and invited his relatives to a meal. After they had eaten, they spent the night there" (Gen 31:54). Other places also indicate it was common to symbolize the ratifying of a covenant with a meal (cf. Gen 26:30; 31:54; Luke 22:15–20). The renewal of the covenant in the postexilic period was also accompanied by a meal (Neh 8–10, esp. 8:9–12).

---

28. Smith, *Lectures on the Religion of the Semites: The Fundamental Institutions*.
29. Ibid., 32.
30. Ibid., 261.
31. MacDonald, *Not Bread Alone: The Uses of Food in the Old Testament*, 4.

Out of this tradition of covenant meals, a new eschatological expectation arose in Second Temple Judaism—the messianic or kingdom banquet.

2.6 The Messianic Banquet

D. S. Russell concludes in his study of Jewish apocalyptic that the idea of an eschatological banquet was "a familiar one" in ancient Judaism.[32] Multiple passages in the Jewish Scriptures (e.g. Isa 49:9-12; 55; 65:13-16; Zech 9:9-17) use the image of a banquet or feast to describe the joy of the coming age of salvation. The most significant of these passages is Isaiah 25:6-9:

> On this mountain the Lord of hosts will make for all peoples
> a feast of rich food, a feast of well-aged wine,
> of rich food full of marrow, of aged wine well refined.
> And he will swallow up on this mountain
> the covering that is cast over all peoples,
> the veil that is spread over all nations.
> He will swallow up death forever;
> and the Lord God will wipe away tears from all faces,
> and the reproach of his people he will take away from all the earth,
> for the Lord has spoken.
> It will be said on that day,
> "Behold, this is our God; we have waited for him, that he might save us.
> This is the Lord; we have waited for him;
> let us be glad and rejoice in his salvation."

Royalty and feasts go together in many ancient contexts.[33] Many mythologies feature sumptuous feasts for the gods. YHWH appears as the host of banquets in the Psalms (23:5; 30:9; 63:6; 65:5; 103:5; 132:15). But YHWH's feast here is for all peoples. He moves beyond his initial choice and issues a universal invitation.

Ordinarily the nations who come to the Lord must bring gifts (cf. Isa 18:7; 60:4-7; Ps 96:8). Here the banquet is pure grace—the nations bring nothing. The food offered was the kind fit for kings.[34]

---

32. Quoted in Pitre, "Jesus, the Messianic Banquet, and the Kingdom of God," 134.

33. Watts, *Isaiah 34-66*, 25, 390.

34. Bailey, *Through Peasant Eyes: A Literary-Cultural Approach to the Parables in Luke*, 93.

It was customary for the king at his banquet to demonstrate his power by a heroic act. Marduk, for example, is pictured as having made a garment disappear and reappear (Enuma Elish IV, 28; ANET, 66).[35] YHWH's demonstrative deed was "to swallow up" (v. 7) the "covering" (a mourning shroud) that lay heavy over all peoples and all nations. The parallelism indicates that the great shroud/veil is death: "The covering that is cast . . . the veil that is spread . . . swallow up death forever." The people swallow the banquet; God swallows up death and the covering. And the veil is not just removed, it is destroyed. Hence the messianic banquet has a strong salvific tone.

The messianic note is struck in verse nine when these events are heralded by one who has been waited for and who brings salvation. The pilgrimage of the nations indicates the ultimate establishment of YHWH's rule, but in the absence of violence. The feast brings together the disparate groups with YHWH as the benevolent host at his own enthronement. Communion and reconciliation become possible, indeed inevitable, in this new era of YHWH's reign.[36] There is no distinction between the nations in this compassion. YHWH also removes the disgrace of Israel (v. 8) as, if all are ruled by YHWH, there is no scope for foreign oppression. Indeed, Israel goes from the periphery to the center within this new kingdom, as it is Israel's God who reigns for all.

The kingdom banquet theme was developed in the intertestamental period especially with respect to the role of the Messiah, but somehow the idea that the Gentiles would be invited to attend came to be muted.[37] In the Qumran community (1QSa 2:11-22), the great banquet was specifically connected with the coming of the Messiah. In the last days, the Messiah will gather with the whole congregation to eat bread and drink wine. The Gentiles are obviously excluded and, along with them, all imperfect Jews. Thus, Isaiah's open-ended vision has been blurred if not eliminated.

This first-century expectation is reflected by the wedding supper of Revelation (Rev 19:9, 17-18) which echoes royal wedding banquets and victory banquets.[38] Victory and consummation for the church and its Lord also spell final defeat and judgment for God's enemies (Rev 19:17-18; cf. Ezek 39:17-20). But the final word is an open, hope-filled invitation (22:17):

---

35. Watts, *Isaiah 34-66*, 25, 391.

36. Crabbe, "Transforming Tables: Meals as Encounters with the Kingdom in Luke."

37. Bailey, *Through Peasant Eyes: A Literary-Cultural Approach to the Parables in Luke*, 90.

38. Ryken et al., *Dictionary of Biblical Imagery*, 828-9.

OLD TESTAMENT BACKGROUND

The Spirit and the Bride say, "Come." And let the one who hears say, "Come." And let the one who is thirsty come; let the one who desires take the water of life without price.

Here is a picture of a great eschatological banquet to which people are invited and marked by abundance. Pitre concludes:

> Both the Old Testament and ancient Jewish literature demonstrate a vibrant expectation of a great eschatological feast that would take place in the age of salvation. In Scripture itself, this banquet would consist of the ingathering of Israel and the Gentiles, the forgiveness of sins, and the overthrow of death. In later Jewish literature, the banquet became directly tied to other ancient hopes, such as the coming of the Messiah, the resurrection of the dead, and even the return to Paradise or to a heavenly promised land.[39]

2.7 Summation

This brief summary of calling, election, covenant, and covenant meals in the OT and the intertestamental period has highlighted the close relationship between these concepts in the mind of first-century Jews like Jesus and Paul. Luke's knowledge of the OT, as reflected by his use of it in his Gospel and Acts, would suggest that he too was aware of these concepts and the relationship between them. The relationship can be summarized in this diagram:

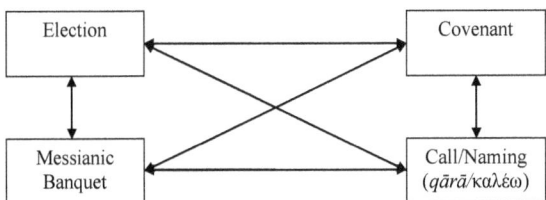

The conflation of these ideas meant that the first-century Jew would have lived in eager expectation of an invitation/call to a great eschatological banquet to be hosted by the Messiah to mark the arrival of salvation for Israel. Although Isaiah envisaged this banquet as being one where the Gentiles would be invited/called, by the first century this expectation had been muted.

---

39. Pitre, "Jesus, the Messianic Banquet, and the Kingdom of God," 160.

It is with this rich background that Jesus, Paul, and Luke use the term καλέω. However, to investigate whether and how these authors used καλέω soteriologically, we must first have an understanding of their soteriologies. In the next chapter, we will examine the unique soteriologies of Luke and Paul.

3

The Soteriologies of Paul and Luke

3.1 Introduction

THE QUESTION FOCUSING AND driving this study is, "What role does the call (καλέω) of God play in the soteriologies of Paul and Luke?" And so, the overall aim is to compare and contrast the role of καλέω and its cognates in the soteriologies of Luke and Paul and to draw conclusions and implications from its use.

In order to commence this investigation, the background to the meaning of καλέω has been undertaken to illuminate what Paul and Luke *could* have meant when they used the word in their writing. In order to determine what it might mean in any given passage, the purpose of the author in that passage must be discerned. This is, of course, not always an easy matter. In this case, one clue to assist in being able to discern the writer's intention in a given passage is to understand the overall soteriology of the author and then consider the usage of καλέω in the light of this soteriology. Hence, this chapter will survey the soteriologies of Paul and Luke in order to be in a better position to determine whether the use of καλέω in a text is soteriological or otherwise. The goal here is not to plumb the depths of Pauline and Lukan soteriology, but simply to provide a platform for an informed investigation of their use of καλέω.

One of the conclusions of this chapter is that the focus on justification in the study of Paul's soteriology, and vicarious atonement in the study of Luke's soteriology, has meant that other categories of salvation have been pushed to the sidelines. In particular, the covenantal aspect of salvation, with its use of the καλέω language, has not received the emphasis it deserves. This chapter will show how covenant, election, and call language are important categories in the soteriology of both Luke and Paul and deserve greater attention.

3.2 The Soteriology of Paul

In Greek, σωτηρία is a general term indicating deliverance of varying kinds.[1] It may be used of healing from disease, safety in travel, or of preservation during times of peril. It may apply to people or things. In the Epistles traditionally attributed to Paul, he uses the verb σῴζω ("to save") twenty-nine times, which is more than any other writer in the NT. He uses the noun σωτήρ ("Savior") twelve times, σωτηρία ("salvation") eighteen times, and σωτήριος ("bringing salvation") once. Clearly, salvation is an important topic for Paul.

The argument in this section with respect to salvation can be summarized by three propositions:

1. Righteousness by faith is a metaphor of salvation, not an all-encompassing term;
2. Covenant deserves a more central place in Pauline soteriology;
3. Righteousness is related to covenant rather than imputation.

By demonstrating the validity of these propositions we will "make room" for καλέω to be examined as a more significant soteriological term in the theology of Paul in two ways. First, it will correct the overemphasis on righteousness/justification in Pauline soteriology. Second, these propositions mean that because of its close association with covenant, καλέω is worthy of more serious examination as a soteriological term.

3.2.1 Righteousness—A Metaphor of Salvation

E. P. Sanders[2] describes Paul's soteriology as "getting in and staying in." Salvation is a transfer from one status to another which has implications for how one should behave. He places many of Paul's terms into the three categories: life outside of Christ, life in Christ, and the transfer terms (salvation terms) which Paul uses to show movement from the first to the second status.

---

1. Morris, "Salvation," 858.
2. Sanders, *Paul, the Law, and the Jewish People*, 6–7.

Sanders argues that humans start in a condemned state but through God's action in Christ they may transfer to the body of those who will be saved. Those who do not transfer face death and destruction. Those who transfer are to live in a certain way. If they transgress, they may experience punishment leading to repentance, or they may be excluded. According to Sanders, salvation is a complex and multifaceted concept for Paul.

A review of the images associated with salvation in Paul's soteriology confirms that Pauline soteriology is a diverse and rich montage. McIver identifies twelve Pauline images of salvation: justification/righteousness, reconciliation, salvation, imputation, honor, grace, through Christ, in Christ, by Christ, sanctification, atonement, and victory.[3] Dunn identifies a list of soteriological metaphors used by Paul and categorizes them in terms of the sources from which they are drawn:[4]

1. Metaphors drawn from the customs of his time:
   a. "justification"
   b. "redemption"
   c. "liberation" and "freedom"
   d. "reconciliation"
   e. "citizenship," "community membership" (Phil 3:20)
   f. transfer into another kingdom (Col 1:13).

2. Metaphors drawn from everyday life:
   a. "salvation"—in the sense of "rescue"
   b. "inheritance" (Gal 3:18)
   c. waking up (Rom 13:11)
   d. night giving way to day (Rom 13:12)
   e. putting off or on clothes, armor (Rom 13:12, 14)
   f. receiving an invitation (καλέω)
   g. writing a letter (2 Cor 3:3).

3. Metaphors drawn from agriculture:
   a. sowing and watering (1 Cor 3:6–8)
   b. irrigation (1 Cor 12:13c)
   c. pitcher of water poured out (Rom 5:5)

3. McIver, "Pauline Images of Salvation."
4. Dunn, *The Theology of Paul the Apostle*, 328–31.

d. grafting (Rom 11:17–24)

   e. harvest (Rom 8:23).

4. Metaphors from commerce:

   a. "seal"—visible stamp of ownership

   b. "first instalment" (2 Cor 1:22)

   c. "into the name of"

   d. "confirm" (1 Cor 1:6, 8)

   e. "tested and approved" (Rom 14:18)

   f. building (1 Cor 3:10–12)

5. Metaphors from religion:

   a. "saints"

   b. "anointing" (2 Cor 1:21)

   c. sacrifice—Jesus' death as a sacrifice

   d. priestly service (Rom 12:1)

   e. access (to the inner sanctum of the cult) (Rom 5:1)

   f. bodies as temples of God's presence (1 Cor 3:16–17)

   g. "circumcision" as descriptive of the work of the cross (Phil 3:3)

   h. ritual cleansing—"washing," "purifying" (1 Cor 6:11)

   i. baptism (Rom 6:3)

   j. "new creation" (2 Cor 5:17).

6. Metaphors from major events of life:

   a. abortion or "premature birth"—or "untimely birth" (1 Cor 15:8)

   b. "becoming your father through the Gospel" (1 Cor 4:15)

   c. "adoption" (Rom 8:15)

   d. engagement with Christ (2 Cor 11:2)

   e. marriage with Christ (1 Cor 6:17)

   f. death, dying, crucifixion (Rom 6:3–6).

However, the Reformers, and those in their tradition, place the concept of righteousness/justification at the center of Pauline soteriology. Ryken writes: "Justification is central to the Christian gospel because it answers the fundamental question, 'How can a sinful human being be righteous before a holy God?'"⁵ He cites a number of Reformers in support of this claim: John Calvin called it "the main hinge on which salvation turns." Cranmer described it as "the strong rock and foundation of Christian religion." Luther called justification "the chief article of Christian doctrine," so that "when justification has fallen, everything has fallen." Ryken concludes: "Whether we think of justification as the hinge, the foundation, or the standing-and-falling article of salvation, there is no hope of salvation without it."

Some see justification as an all-encompassing soteriological concept:

> The righteousness of God is an all-encompassing act that implements the entire plan of salvation, including justification, redemption, atonement, forgiveness, membership in the new covenant community, reconciliation, the gift of the Holy Spirit, power for new obedience, union with Christ, freedom from sin, and vindication at the final judgement.⁶

Certainly, righteousness deserves its place as a central doctrine in soteriology. It is often synonymous with "salvation" in OT and Jewish literature (Judg 5:11; 1 Sam 12:7; Isa 56:1) and the term is located within the OT contexts of creation and covenant. God wishes to establish his righteousness throughout all the earth (Gen 18:25; Ps 98:9) and in saving Israel he also acts righteously because he is faithful to his covenant promises.

However, to say justification is the "hinge, the foundation, or the standing-and-falling article of salvation" overstates its importance. Paul uses a variety of metaphors to express as fully as possible a reality which defies a simple or uniform description.⁷ Consequently, it would be wrong to take one metaphor as primary or normative as has happened with justification in Protestant theology. Paul offers us "not theories but vivid metaphors."⁸ As Dunn says, "It is an unfortunate kind of sophistication which believes that the only thing to do with metaphors is to turn them into theories."⁹

Building on the work of Theissen,¹⁰ Beker¹¹ reaches similar conclusions. Paul's soteriological metaphors (physical transformation, death and life, unification liberation, justification, and reconciliation) overlap with one another, cohere with one another, and are therefore useful in interpreting one another. But every metaphor has its limitations; hence the need for

---

5. Ryken, *Justification*, 8.
6. Bird, *Introducing Paul: The Man, His Mission and His Message*, 94.
7. Grams, "Contextualisation, Intertextuality, and Paul's Soteriology," 6.
8. Fitzmyer, *Paul and His Theology: A Brief Sketch*, 65f.
9. Dunn, *The Theology of Paul the Apostle*, 333.
10. Theissen, "Soteriologische Symbolik in Den Paulinischen Schriften."
11. Beker, *Paul the Apostle: The Triumph of God in Life and Thought*, 256f.

overlapping and multiple metaphors.[12] Paul's theology cannot be described by one metaphor. To do so would limit his theology and press a single metaphor into too great a service.

The application of the metaphor of justification to encapsulate Paul's soteriology is an artificial imposition. For instance, Sanders correctly distinguishes between the "center of Paul's thought" and the central terminology he uses to describe the transfer from the unsaved to saved state. He emphasizes that in discussing "dying with Christ" and "righteousness by faith," he is discussing terminology, not Paul's conception of how one enters the body of Christ.[13] Given the complexity and diversity of Paul's terminology, attempts to encapsulate "Paul's thought" must be considered with caution. It is useful to be able to neatly summarize Paul's soteriology, but it may not be possible to do so.

3.2.2 Covenant Is an Important Part of Pauline Soteriology

An increasing awareness of the importance of covenant in Pauline soteriology has been a consequence of the New Perspective on Paul (NPP). The basis of the NPP is an improved understanding of Second Temple Judaism. James Dunn was the first to use the term "The New Perspective" in the 1983 Manson Memorial Lecture, *The New Perspective on Paul and the Law*.[14] However, E. P. Sanders in *Paul and Palestinian Judaism* had earlier argued that the Judaism of Paul's day was not a religion of "works-salvation" but a religion of grace:

> On the point at which many have found the decisive contrast between Paul and Judaism—grace and works—Paul is in agreement with Palestinian Judaism . . . Salvation is by grace but judgment is according to works . . . God saves by grace, but . . . within the framework established by grace he rewards good deeds and punishes transgression.[15]

The Reformation perspective has Paul arguing against a legalistic Jewish culture (somewhat like their argument against the Roman Catholic Church) that advocated salvation through works. However, the NPP posits

---

12. Grams, "Contextualisation, Intertextuality, and Paul's Soteriology," 6.
13. Sanders, *Paul, the Law, and the Jewish People*, 5.
14. Dunn, "The New Perspective on Paul."
15. Sanders, *Paul and Palestinian Judaism: A Comparison of Patterns of Religion*, 543.

that Paul was actually combating Jews who were boasting that salvation came through their ethnic identity.

Sanders argues that the essence of Second Temple and Rabbinic Judaism was "covenantal nomism."[16] This is the view that salvation is established on the basis of the covenant and that the covenant requires the proper response of obedience to its commandments, while also providing a means of atonement for transgression. Hence when Jews required strict obedience to the law, it was because they were keeping the covenant, rather than earning their way into the covenant. The emphasis on obedience was in the context of covenant compliance and not legalism. It was not their works that helped them attain salvation, but their "nationalistic boundary markers" (i.e. circumcision, food laws, Sabbath, etc.) that kept them within the people of God. "Works of the law" were not seen either by his Jewish adversaries, or by Paul himself, as works which earned God's favor. They were rather seen as badges: simply what membership of the covenant people involved and what marked out the Jews as God's people.

Hence, in his Epistles, Paul is linking salvation to membership of a covenant consummated by the blood of Jesus. Further, he is not fighting legalism, but the works and national pride that separated the Jews from the Gentiles. Paul opposed the circumcision party, not because of "legalism" or "works-righteousness," but because of what Wright calls "national righteousness"—the belief that fleshly Jewish descent guarantees membership in God's true covenant people.[17]

However, it must be acknowledged that neither Luke nor Paul mention covenant often. There are only eight occurrences of διαθήκη (covenant) in the letters that are generally accepted as Pauline: Romans 9:4; 11:27; 1 Corinthians 11:25; 2 Corinthians 3:6, 14; Galatians 3:15, 17; 4:24 (cf. also Eph 2:12). Dunn[18] argues that covenant is therefore a "peripheral" feature of Paul's theology on the basis of the infrequent and reactive nature of Paul's usage of διαθήκη.

Certainly, Paul does not use covenant language frequently, but what is generally presumed need not always be explicitly stated. Dunn's approach makes the mistake of equating words and concepts. Reflecting Barr's[19] criticism of such a narrow reproach, Porter writes, "One cannot, and should not, simply equate the concept of covenant with a single lexical item in the

---

16. Ibid., 75.
17. Wright, "The Paul of History and the Apostle of Faith," 65.
18. Dunn, "Did Paul Have a Covenant Theology? Reflections on Romans 9:4 and 11:27."
19. Barr, *The Semantics of Biblical Language*.

language."[20] Hence, Porter conducted a study based on the semantic domain of covenant through the use of the Louw-Nida lexicon. He concludes that there is a semantic relationship between διαθήκη and "righteousness" and "promise" words. δικαιοσύνη language belongs "in the context of covenant relation rather than in the context of legal procedures."[21] Hence the language of "promise" which appears in Galatians 3, and in Romans 4 and 9, is also related to covenant. For example:

> For the promise to Abraham and his offspring that he would be heir of the world did not come through the law but through the righteousness of faith (Rom 4:13).

Covenantal relationship is also implied in Paul addressing the Romans in 1:7 as ἀγαπητοῖς θεοῦ ("beloved [of God]") and, as we shall see in chapter 4, κλητοῖς ἁγίοις ("called [to be] saints").[22]

And, of course, Paul *does* explicitly refer to the Abrahamic, Mosaic and "new" covenants in his writings. In Galatians 3:15–17, he argues for the priority and inviolability of the Abrahamic covenant:

> To give a human example, brothers: even with a man-made covenant (διαθήκην), no one annuls it or adds to it once it has been ratified. Now the promises were made to Abraham and to his offspring. It does not say, "And to offsprings," referring to many, but referring to one, "And to your offspring," who is Christ. This is what I mean: the law, which came 430 years afterward, does not annul a covenant previously ratified by God, so as to make the promise void.

Paul uses his rabbinic expertise to drive home the idea that legalism and God's gracious promise are rooted in two very different perspectives. The argument at 3:15 is based on an analogy taken from the law courts.[23] A covenant (διαθήκη), or will, that has been ratified cannot be annulled. In the same way, the law associated with the Mosaic covenant does not set aside the promise of the Abrahamic covenant. This was consistent with Paul's understanding of the overlap of the covenants.

In Romans 9:4–5 Paul lists the covenant as one of the privileges belonging to Israel, along with sonship, glory, the giving of the law, worship, the promises, and the patriarchs. It appears that here Paul also has the

---

20. Porter, "The Concept of Covenant in Paul," 284.

21. Louw and Nida, *Greek-English Lexicon of the New Testament: Based on Semantic Domains*, 2, 452.

22. Campbell, "Covenant and New Covenant."

23. Mohrlang and Borchert, *Cornerstone Biblical Commentary*, 294.

Abrahamic covenant primarily in view. The focus is on the call and election of Abraham who in Romans 4 was depicted as a paradigm of the believer.

In Romans 11, Paul combines Isaiah 59:12 and Isaiah 27:9 to describe a future redemption for Israel despite her present refusal of the gospel: "This will be my covenant (διαθήκη) with them, when I take away their sins" (Rom 11:27). The argument concerning the olive tree, and the theme of Romans 11 generally, is that despite the present enmity towards the gospel, the election/call of Israel still stands. "God has not rejected his people whom he foreknew" (Rom 11:2). The covenant is secure and Israel's election/call is not in doubt, for "the gifts and the call of God are irrevocable" (Rom 11:29).[24]

Paul also refers to a divine covenant in 1 Corinthians 11:25 where he gives the rendering of Jesus' words at the Last Supper as "this cup is the new covenant (καινὴ διαθήκη) in my blood." As Beale and Carson point out:

> Jesus' statement that the cup "is the new covenant in my blood" fuses together the language of Jer. 31:31 ("a new covenant") and Exod. 24:8 ("the blood of the covenant that the Lord has made with you"). The latter text refers to the establishment of the covenant at Sinai, while the former consists of God's promise to establish a new covenant in the time of postexilic restoration. By fusing the two texts together, Jesus interprets his impending death as the sacrifice that establishes the new covenant associated with the second exodus.[25]

To summarize, it must be acknowledged that Paul did not frequently use explicit covenant terminology. However, there are frequent allusions to the covenant through related terms. As Porter has demonstrated, using Louw and Nida's lexical approach, limiting Paul's understanding of covenant to the use of διαθήκη, is unjustified. "Promise" and "justify" are also covenant terminology. In addition, when Paul does use διαθήκη it occurs at crucial points in his writings such as his account of the Last Supper.

And so, even though Paul does not refer explicitly to covenant frequently, it is an important part of his soteriology. Paul sees Christ as the fulfillment of the OT covenants. The death of Christ is a sacrifice that establishes a new covenant in the tradition of the OT covenants bringing salvation to both Jew and Gentile.

This new perspective on Judaism and Paul has implications for the understanding of Paul's soteriology. The NPP has effectively moved the covenant plan of God closer to the center of Pauline soteriology. As a

---

24. Campbell, "Covenant and New Covenant," 181.

25. Beale and Carson, *Commentary on the New Testament Use of the Old Testament*, 736.

consequence, the overwhelming importance of the doctrine of the imputation of righteousness is brought into question.

3.2.3 Righteousness Is Related to Covenant Rather Than Imputation

The reformed view holds that a person can only be declared righteous/justified by means of a righteousness that is "imputed" to a person on the basis of the vicarious and substitutionary death of Christ (see Gal 3:22; Rom 3:22, 26; Phil 3:9). The righteousness of Christ is imputed to the believer through union with him. "Imputation is a synthetic way of holding together a number of themes that clearly point in the direction of imputation, or something very much akin to it."[26]

However, a better understanding of the importance of covenant in Paul's soteriology, as discussed above, means that when he speaks of "righteousness from/of God" (δικαιοσύνη θεοῦ) in Romans 3:22, he is referring less to something which is imputed and more to God's own righteousness. The "righteousness of God" is God's "covenant fidelity." The creator of the world, who established his covenant with Abraham, has now fulfilled that covenant in Christ. In his own righteousness, God enables people to become righteous: "For our sake he made him to be sin who knew no sin, so that in him we might become the righteousness of God" (2 Cor 5:21). In his faithfulness to his people God has provided Christ as the propitiation for sins (Rom 3:21–26) so that he, and they, may live in uninterrupted covenant fellowship. By the work of the Spirit we are united with Christ and become God's righteousness in Christ, and on that basis, God the judge pronounces us righteous and entitled to the full privileges of covenant membership. These actions embody God's covenant faithfulness.[27] Justification is not the *means* whereby it becomes possible to declare someone in the right but is the *declaration* itself that someone is in the covenant.[28]

Wright argues that it makes no sense to say that a judge imputes, imparts, bequeaths, conveys, or otherwise transfers his righteousness to either the plaintiff or the defendant. "Righteousness is not an object, a substance or a gas which can be passed across the courtroom."[29] Instead,

> "Justification" in the first century was not about how someone might establish a relationship with God. It was about God's

---

26. Bird, *Introducing Paul: The Man, His Mission and His Message*, 97.
27. Garlington, *Studies in the New Perspective on Paul: Essays and Reviews*, 30.
28. Dumbrell, "Justification and the New Covenant," 17.
29. Wright, *What Saint Paul Really Said*, 98.

eschatological definition, both future and present of who was, in fact, a member of his people. In Sanders' terms, it was not so much about "getting in," or indeed about "staying in," as about "how you could tell who was in." In standard Christian theological language, it wasn't so much about soteriology as about ecclesiology; not so much about salvation as about the church.[30]

The downplaying of the idea that righteousness is something that is imputed at the moment of conversion has, understandably, caused concern for some scholars. Piper says Wright's "portrayal of the gospel and of the doctrine of justification in particular is so disfigured that it becomes difficult to recognize as biblically faithful."[31] Less dramatically, Hassler concludes that within the increasing trajectory toward a covenantal understanding of justification within Pauline scholarship since the emergence of the NPP, there still remains significant evidence that justification, at its core, is concerned with the individual who is counted righteous apart from any human works.[32]

However, the insights from the NPP cannot be ignored. Indeed, they bring an added richness to our understanding of Paul's soteriology as a multifaceted phenomenon. Justification remains a crucial element in our understanding of salvation, but a number of other elements, including covenant membership, complement it.

An important consequence of the NPP is a greater appreciation of the communal dimensions of salvation implied in covenant belonging:

> That there was such a personal dimension need not be denied, but it existed within and not separated from a communal and, indeed, a cosmic dimension. Paul's doctrine of justification by faith was not solely and not primarily oriented towards the individual but to the interpretation of the people of God. The justified man was "in Christ," which is a communal concept. And, necessarily because it was eschatological, the doctrine moved towards the salvation of the world, a new creation.[33]

This emphasis on the communal dimensions of salvation will be highlighted when we examine the Paul's usage of call language in chapter 4.

---

30. Ibid., 119.

31. Piper, *The Future of Justification: A Response to N. T. Wright*, 15.

32. Hassler, "Justification and the Individual in the Wake of the New Perspective on Paul."

33. Davies, "Paul: From the Jewish Point of View," 715–6.

3.2.4 *Summation*

The Reformation brought a justifiable emphasis on the imputation of righteousness as the grounds of salvation. However, the unintended consequence of this emphasis has been the downplaying of other categories of salvation. In their attempts to simplify the message of the gospel, evangelicals may also have overemphasized imputation of righteousness at the expense of other perspectives on salvation such as entering the kingdom of God or participating in the new covenant.

Integrating the NPP into discussions of Pauline soteriology allows a deeper and richer understanding of salvation. The new understanding of Second Temple Judaism and the diversity of the metaphors that Paul uses to describe salvation mean that the description of Paul's soteriology must remain multifaceted. Systematization remains helpful but restraint in reaching neat formulas, even for the sake of evangelism, must be exercised.

It would be wrong to argue that covenant is the center of Paul's soteriology, just as it would be wrong to argue that justification is. However, the place of covenant membership in salvation, and with it the concept of call, deserve a higher place in our understanding of Pauline soteriology. Covenant membership is more than an implication or result of justification, but is intrinsically bound up with salvation itself: God's righteousness is his saving activity in establishing justice throughout *creation*, fulfilling the *covenant* with Israel, manifested in *Christ*, and culminating at the *consummation*.[34] As Bird points out, this conclusion is not a "theological fudge to satisfy all and sundry"[35] but a proper understanding of Paul's articulation of justification based on both the Reformed view and the New Perspective. Further, the question of what comes first, "forensic status" or "covenant membership," is much like asking about the priority of the chicken or the egg. Both aspects must be integrated for a comprehensive understanding of justification, and for that matter, salvation.

3.3 The Soteriology of Luke

The aim of this chapter is to provide the soteriological backgrounds of Paul and Luke in which their respective use of καλέω may be situated. Much of the scholarship on Lukan soteriology has focused on the role of Christ's atoning death. However, it will be argued in this section that if one seeks

---

34. Bird, "Justification as Forensic Declaration and Covenant Membership: A *Via Media* between Reformed and Revisionist Readings of Paul," 129.

35. Ibid., 110.

to simply focus on Luke's own emphases, the kingdom of God and the covenants emerge as the key features of Luke's soteriology. If this is the case his use of καλέω in a soteriological sense is therefore quite apt (as demonstrated in chapter 2), although yet to be demonstrated.

Luke's soteriology, though clearly an important part of his theology, has at times been viewed as something of an "ugly stepchild."[36] This is because Luke appears to show the "what" of salvation without as much attention to the "how," and even omitting, in the opinion of many scholars like Conzelmann, any significant reference to Christ's atoning death. The majority view of scholarship is that the death of Jesus as an innocent martyr provides the best explanation of atonement in Luke.[37]

However, it must be said that,

> Despite the low-keyed interpretation the death of Jesus traditionally has received in Lukan scholarship, there can be no doubt about the prominent place it occupies in Luke–Acts in terms of the statements made about it. These statements unequivocally assign to Jesus' death a place of divine necessity in God's salvation plan, although at first glance it is not always clear what exactly this means.[38]

In order to summarize the huge breadth of scholarship, the discussion will start with the meaning and use of the salvation words in Luke. The major trajectories of Lukan soteriology as identified by Timothy Reardon will then be used as a framework for the analysis of the opinions.

3.3.1 Salvation in Luke

Luke uses the language of salvation more than the other evangelists: the noun "salvation" (σωτηρία) is found seven times (never in Mark or Matthew); God and Jesus are "Savior" (σωτήρ, 1:47; 2:11—never in Mark or Matthew); and the verb "save" (σῴζω) is used seventeen times (Mark thirteen times; Matthew fourteen times), sometimes in the sense "heal" (e.g. 8:48, 50), but often in a spiritual sense (e.g. 7:50; 8:12; 13:23; 19:10—all unique to Luke). There are a further twenty-seven uses of this word group in

---

36. Reardon, "Recent Trajectories and Themes in Lukan Soteriology," 77.

37. Ibid., 87.

38. van Zyl, "The Soteriological Meaning of Jesus' Death in Luke–Acts: A Survey of Possibilities."

Acts. Luke particularly emphasizes that salvation is for all, notably through his focus on Gentiles, Samaritans and marginalized people within Israel.[39]

This demonstrates that salvation, especially its extension to the Gentiles, is a major interest of Luke. However, the exact nature of salvation in Luke–Acts is much debated.

3.3.2 Trajectories of Lukan Soteriology

Reardon identifies four major trajectories in Lukan soteriology.[40] The first follows the direction of Hans Conzelmann. In his seminal 1954 work, *Die Mitte der Zeit (The Middle of Time)*, translated into English as *The Theology of St. Luke*,[41] Conzelmann asserts that the author of Luke–Acts has developed a theology based primarily on the apparent delay of the Parousia. Faced with this prolonged delay of Jesus' return, Luke created a tripartite salvation-historical scheme with three distinct epochs: the time before Jesus, the "middle" (*Mitte*) period of Jesus that is marked by the appearance of salvation, and the time of the church in anticipation of Jesus' (and salvation's) return. However, during the period of the church, salvation is something remembered and expected rather than experienced. In this sense, it is "spiritualized." The church endures suffering in the same manner as Jesus, who died an innocent martyr's death. Since, in Conzelmann's opinion, Luke does not explain the means of reconciliation or atonement, the death of Christ has no direct soteriological significance or connection to forgiveness of sins.

In the same trajectory, I. Howard Marshall concurs that the central theme in the writings of Luke is salvation.[42] But rather than relegating salvation to the past, Marshall says, "It is more correct to say that Luke has broadened out the time of the End so that it begins with the ministry of Jesus, includes the time of the church, and is consummated at the *parousia*."[43] For Marshall, there is a spiritual form of salvation in the present that does not directly relate to the reversal of social or economic conditions. Like Conzelmann, Marshall asserts that Lukan economic and social reversal is delayed until the eschaton.

---

39. Wenham and Walton, *Exploring the New Testament*, 248.

40. Reardon, "Recent Trajectories and Themes in Lukan Soteriology." This section draws heavily on Reardon's work.

41. Conzelmann, *The Theology of St. Luke*.

42. Marshall, *Luke: Historian and Theologian*, 116.

43. Ibid., 110.

The second trajectory has attempted to identify a non-expiatory Lukan means of salvation.[44] These writers argue that although Luke does not favor sacrificial metaphors for the death of Jesus, there are other metaphors that he utilizes which are just as effective. It is certainly plausible that Luke had a soteriological scheme that did not depend on the expiatory death of Jesus. Isaiah, whom Luke draws on significantly, has salvation as God redeeming people without a price, taking the initiative for reconciliation (e.g., Isa 43:1; 52:3; 63:9). Doble, who identifies Christ with the suffering righteous one in the Wisdom of Solomon and the imitation of Christ in discipleship as the appropriation of salvation, is another example of this trajectory.[45]

The third trajectory of Lukan soteriology seeks a more holistic salvation that incorporates the physical, social, economic, political, and spiritual. Within this trajectory is Joel Green.[46] This trajectory identifies salvation as incorporation into the Christocentric community and rescue from enemies (including cosmic, demonic forces, and worldly patronage systems), reception of the Holy Spirit, and forgiveness of sins. The theme of reversal is demonstrated most fully in the death of Jesus, fulfilling the prophecy of Isaiah's Suffering Servant.[47] This trajectory concludes that Luke does not attach atoning significance to the death of Jesus. So, the Last Supper does not demonstrate eucharistic qualities but is an eschatological meal—the fulfillment of the kingdom of God. The cross represents opposition that ultimately leads to the propagation of the gospel, a model for true discipleship, and a representation of lowliness associated with the curse of God in Deuteronomy 21:22–23.

The fourth and final trajectory attempts to identify that the expiatory death of Jesus *is* a component of Luke–Acts.[48] These studies tend to focus on Luke's record of the Last Supper and its allusion to the vicarious sacrifice of Jesus.[49] Of course, these approaches presuppose the necessity of substitutionary atonement as the only meaningful theological soteriological scheme.[50]

The number and variation of these trajectories of Lukan soteriology suggest that it is a diverse and complex subject which has primarily focused

---

44. Reardon, "Recent Trajectories and Themes in Lukan Soteriology," 83.
45. Doble, *The Paradox of Salvation: Luke's Theology of the Cross.*
46. Green, *The Theology of the Gospel of Luke*, 64–65.
47. Reardon, "Recent Trajectories and Themes in Lukan Soteriology," 85.
48. Ibid., 86.
49. du Plessis, "The Saving Significance of Jesus and His Death on the Cross in Luke's Gospel: Focusing on Luke 22: 19b–20."
50. Reardon, "Recent Trajectories and Themes in Lukan Soteriology," 87.

on the vicarious death of Christ. Van Zyl is correct when he says: "In light of the scholarly debate it must be said at the outset that Jesus' death in Luke–Acts cannot be summed up in a single monolithic view, but is best described in terms of different perspectives."[51] Without downplaying the importance of the debate, the arguments about the role of Christ's death have tended to dominate and perhaps even distort the study of Luke's soteriology.

An alternative approach to entering the debate over Reardon's trajectories is to consider Lukan soteriology in the light of the OT and to consider what he does say, rather than what he may not. As Conzelmann demonstrated, Luke is especially keen to show that Christ and his church are an integral part of God's broader tripartite salvation-historical scheme. In the next section it will be argued that two concepts are close to the core of Luke's soteriology because of their role in salvation history: the kingdom of God and the covenants. These concepts make more room for καλέω to be considered more seriously as a soteriological term than the debates on the expiatory nature of Christ's death would allow.

3.3.3 Salvation and the Kingdom of God

One of the few things that most NT scholars agree about is that the kingdom of God is close to the center of Jesus' teachings. Powell demonstrates that salvation in Luke–Acts means participation in the reign of God.[52] Given the importance of YHWH's kingship and his saving work for Israel in the OT, this is not surprising. The Jewish mind typically associated salvation with deliverance from enemies, while Greco-Romans thought of salvation more as the bestowal of various blessings. Luke demonstrates that the kingdom brings positive dimensions (peace, blessing, and eternal life) and the removal of negative ones (disease, demons, sin). By including both dimensions in his presentation of salvation, Luke does justice to both the Hebrew and Greek backgrounds out of which he writes.[53]

Whether the healings and social reversals described in Luke are only during the "middle time" or not, they demonstrate that the kingdom of God is about salvation. A key verse is Luke 18:24–26 where the two are used in parallel:

---

51. van Zyl, "The Soteriological Meaning of Jesus' Death in Luke–Acts: A Survey of Possibilities," 536.

52. This section draws extensively on Powell, "Salvation in Luke–Acts."

53. Ibid., 7.

> Jesus, seeing that he had become sad, said, "How difficult it is for those who have wealth to enter the kingdom of God! For it is easier for a camel to go through the eye of a needle than for a rich person to enter the kingdom of God." Those who heard it said, "Then who can be saved?"

For Luke, salvation was also a here-and-now expression of the kingdom of God to Jew, marginalized, and Gentile.

The relationship between kingdom and salvation is forged through the function of the Messiah. Luke presents Jesus as both Messiah *and* Savior: "For unto you is born this day in the city of David a Savior (σωτήρ) who is Christ (χριστὸς) the Lord" (Luke 2:11). When John the Baptist asks whether he is the Messiah, Jesus replies in Luke 7:22:

> Go back and report to John what you have seen and heard: The blind receive sight, the lame walk, those who have leprosy are cleansed, the deaf hear, the dead are raised, and the good news is proclaimed to the poor.

As *Messiah*, Jesus is the one who fulfils God's promises to Israel (Luke 4:16-21; 24:27-41). As *Savior* he brings healing, peace, and forgiveness of sins (Acts 4:9-10; 10:38). The two are brought together in various places:

> When the crowds learned it, they followed him, and he welcomed them and spoke to them of the kingdom of God and cured those who had need of healing (Luke 9:11).

> Heal the sick in it and say to them, "The kingdom of God has come near to you" (Luke 10:9).

Through encounters with the Messiah, people are saved from things that prevent them from living life as God intends and so, are enabled to participate in God's kingdom. In presenting salvation as participation in the reign of God, Luke makes no distinction between the physical, spiritual, or social aspects of salvation: "Which is easier, to say, 'Your sins are forgiven you,' or to say, 'Rise and walk'?" (Luke 5:23). God is concerned with all aspects of human life and relationships so salvation may involve the putting right of any aspect that is not as it should be. Participation in the reign of God is a present possibility that involves salvation from anything that prevents one from living life as God intends.

Hence, according to Luke, salvation, which is participation in the reign of God, is available to all. This salvation is available because God has granted the vindicated Messiah the right to bestow salvation on whomever he chooses (elects). And the Messiah chooses to bestow salvation on the marginalized Jews and Gentiles as well. People who wish to participate in the reign of God receive this salvation when, through God's grace, they respond to the proclaimed word about Jesus with repentance and faith.

Even though Luke may not expound a theory of the atonement he describes the basis for salvation in the kingdom: the life of Jesus the Messiah has saving significance because it is in the life of Jesus the Messiah that God's kingdom reign is inaugurated and made manifest on earth.

3.3.4 Salvation and the Covenants

Alongside the kingdom of God, covenant is another major feature of Lukan soteriology. Again, this is not surprising as his kingly rule and covenants form the basis of YHWH's whole relationship with Israel. The demand presented to Pharaoh to let Israel go is the demand of the lawful king over against the usurper. The covenant with Israel is the covenant which affirms the suzerainty of YHWH over his people. In the conquest of Canaan, YHWH as king apportions to his people a country; a country, which he, as the creator and king of the earth, can use as he pleases.

Kovacs[54] demonstrates that the covenant concept is foundational to Luke–Acts, as it is central even in the structure of the text. It is at the Gospel's beginning (Luke 1–4), at its ending (Luke 22), at the beginning of Acts (Acts 2), in the middle of Acts (Acts 7 and 13), and in its conclusion (Acts 26). Toward the climactic end of Luke's Gospel, the Lord's Supper narrative records the new covenant established by Jesus in the context of the Passover.

There are four explicit references to the covenant in Luke–Acts:[55] The first is in Luke 1:67–73:

> And his father Zechariah was filled with the Holy Spirit and prophesied, saying,
> "Blessed be the Lord God of Israel,
>   for he has visited and redeemed his people
> and has raised up a horn of salvation for us
>   in the house of his servant David,
> as he spoke by the mouth of his holy prophets from of old,
> that we should be saved from our enemies
>   and from the hand of all who hate us;
> to show the mercy promised to our fathers

---

54. Kovács, "The Covenant Concept as an Organising Principle in Luke–Acts."
55. For an extensive summary, see "The Covenant in Luke–Acts."

and to remember his holy covenant (διαθήκης),
the oath that he swore to our father Abraham, to grant us
that we, being delivered from the hand of our enemies,
might serve him without fear,
in holiness and righteousness before him all our days.

The activity of God in salvation is highlighted in the hymn.[56] God is the one looking favorably, redeeming his people, raising up a mighty Savior, promising and showing mercy, remembering and fulfilling his holy covenant, and granting salvation. The notion of covenant sits squarely in the broader realm of God's saving activities.

The covenant is also explicitly mentioned in the Last Supper (Luke 22:14–23):

> And when the hour came, he reclined at table, and the apostles with him. And he said to them, "I have earnestly desired to eat this Passover with you before I suffer. For I tell you I will not eat it until it is fulfilled in the kingdom of God." And he took a cup, and when he had given thanks he said, "Take this, and divide it among yourselves. For I tell you that from now on I will not drink of the fruit of the vine until the kingdom of God comes." And he took bread, and when he had given thanks, he broke it and gave it to them, saying, "This is my body, which is given for you. Do this in remembrance of me." And likewise the cup after they had eaten, saying, "This cup that is poured out for you is the new covenant (διαθήκη) in my blood. But behold, the hand of him who betrays me is with me on the table. For the Son of Man goes as it has been determined, but woe to that man by whom he is betrayed!" And they began to question one another, which of them it could be who was going to do this.

The four accounts of the Last Supper in the NT fall into two distinct groups representing two specific forms of the tradition.[57] These are Matthew 26:26–29/Mark 14:22–25 and Luke 22:15–20/1 Corinthians 11:23–26. The two forms may be characterized as follows:

Matthew/Mark	Luke/1 Corinthians
"blessed" bread	"give thanks" bread
"Take"	[lack "Take"]

---

56. Ibid., 42.
57. Stein, "Last Supper."

"this is my body"	"this is my body" + "which is ... you"
[lack "This do in my remembrance"]	"This do in my remembrance"
"this"	"this cup"
"thanks" before cup	[lack "thanks" before cup]
reference to all drinking of the cup	[lack reference to all drinking of the cup]
"my blood of the covenant"	"new covenant in my blood"
"which is poured out for many"	Luke has "which is poured out for you" [not in 1 Cor]

The Lukan account is the most unusual of the four. It appears Luke particularly wants to draw attention to the cup of the new covenant. Unlike the other accounts of the Last Supper, Luke mentions a cup before (v. 17), as well as after (v. 20), the bread. He also identifies the cup with the "new covenant" of Jeremiah 31:31–34, while Matthew and Mark point to Exodus 24.

However, Jeremiah 31 is not the only covenant in view in Luke's Last Supper account.[58] The Second Temple Judaism view of the covenants—that they overlapped and complemented one another (see section 2.4)—means that by referring to one covenant Luke was in fact alluding to all the covenants. Luke's allusion to Jeremiah's new covenant prophecy neither excludes the possibility of reference to Exodus 24, nor prevents him elsewhere from explaining Christ's death in relation to the Mosaic economy.

Indeed, for many scholars a relationship between the Mosaic covenant and the synoptic description of the death of Christ is "undeniable."[59] This is regardless of whether the death of Christ is considered vicarious or not. In Exodus 24, where the contracting of a covenant between YHWH and Israel is described, the slaughter of an ox is described along with the sacrifice and the covenant-meal. The blood of the ox was sprinkled against the altar of YHWH to point to his participation in the ritual. The covenant is called "a covenant of blood" (Exod 24:8). The NT descriptions of the Last Supper reflect the same covenant ritual. There is the covenant meal (the Last Supper), the sacrifice itself (Jesus Christ), and the sacrifice action (Christ on the cross). Fensham concludes: "A clearer connection with Exodus 24 could not be expected and furthermore, a clearer reference to the institution of a covenant between the Lord and His people is unthinkable."[60]

---

58. Duncan, "Covenant in the Synoptics, Acts and Pauline Writings."

59. Fensham, "The Covenant as Giving Expression to the Relationship between the Old and New Testament," 91–92.

60. Ibid., 91.

It is also notable that Luke mentions the future kingdom at the beginning of the supper (22:16) rather than at the end as in the other accounts. This placement again reflects a desire to emphasize the links between the Last Supper through the old covenant Passover to the eschatological covenant meal. Just as the "blood of the covenant" in the liturgy of Sinai enabled the Israelites to enter into God's realm, so too at the Last Supper "the blood of the covenant" that is poured out as wine, enables the twelve disciples to eat and drink with Jesus in his kingdom.[61]

The reference to the "hour" (22:14) in which Jesus sat down with his disciples to eat the Passover meal (22:15) also alludes to a stipulation in Exodus 12:8: "They shall eat the lamb that same night; they shall eat it roasted over the fire with unleavened bread and bitter herbs." Whereas this allusion is historical and social in nature, Jesus' assertion in 22:16 that he will not eat the Passover meal again "until it is fulfilled in the kingdom of God" makes a theological point: Jesus fuses the Jewish hopes for a "new exodus" in the future messianic deliverance with his message of the dawn of the kingdom of God in the present, which will be consummated in the future.[62]

Throughout the later chapters of Luke's Gospel the term "salvation" is drawn from Jewish eschatological expectation, and Luke is very likely indebted to a liturgical tradition for the precise formulations.[63] The Last Supper is an eschatological meal—the fulfillment of the kingdom of God. Hicks comments: "Luke places this new covenant meal on the trajectory of redemptive history where the goal is the eschatological community of God in the heavenly kingdom."[64]

Jeremias can identify a strong relationship between these two soteriological terms in his analysis of the Lord's Supper:

> Jesus describes His death as this Eschatological Passover sacrifice: his vicarious (ὑπέρ) death, brings into operation the final deliverance, the New Covenant of God. διαθήκη ("covenant") is a correlation of βασιλεία τῶν οὐρανῶν ("Kingdom of heaven").[65]

The Last Supper is both a pointer to the Mosaic covenant, the kingdom, and the eschatological Messianic banquet. It is a "now-and-not-yet" expression of the covenant banquet.

Luke also refers explicitly to the covenant three times in Acts:

61. Pitre, "Jesus, the Messianic Banquet, and the Kingdom of God," 167–70.
62. Beale and Carson, *Commentary on the New Testament Use of the Old Testament*, 381.
63. Martin, "Salvation and Discipleship in Luke's Gospel," 377–8.
64. Hicks, "The Lord's Table: A Covenant Meal," 5–6.
65. Jeremias, *The Eucharistic Words of Jesus*, 226.

> Acts 3:25: You are the sons of the prophets and of the covenant that God made with your fathers, saying to Abraham, "And in your offspring shall all the families of the earth be blessed."

> Acts 7:8: And he gave him the covenant of circumcision. And so Abraham became the father of Isaac, and circumcised him on the eighth day, and Isaac became the father of Jacob, and Jacob of the twelve patriarchs.

> Acts 7:44: Our ancestors had the tabernacle of the covenant law with them in the wilderness. It had been made as God directed Moses, according to the pattern he had seen.

Reporting these sermons of Peter and Stephen, Luke refers specifically to the Abrahamic and Mosaic covenants, highlighting their importance in the relationship between the Lord and Israel. On both occasions, Peter and Stephen redirect their hearers to the Abrahamic covenant because their ancestral rejection of, and disobedience to, Moses.

In addition to these explicit references, there are also a number of implicit references to the covenants in Luke–Acts. Klaus Baltzer[66] identifies four features of treaties in the ancient Near East:

1. Antecedent History
2. Statement of Substance Concerning the Future Relationship
3. Specific Stipulations
4. Curses and Blessings

With these features in mind Kovács identifies a number of implicit references to these features in Luke–Acts.[67] For example, Luke 1:32–33 reflects the statements of antecedent history and the future relationship present in the ancient Near East treaties:

> He will be great and will be called the Son of the Most High.
> And the Lord God will give to him the throne of his father

---

66. Baltzer, *The Covenant Formulary in Old Testament, Jewish and Early Christian Writings*, 9–10.

67. Luke 1:32–33, Davidic covenant; 1:72–75, Abrahamic covenant; 2:30–32, Isaiah 42:6/49:6 and Isaianic servant covenant; 3:4–6, Isaiah 40:3–5 and covenant restoration; 4:18–19; 4:24–27, Isaiah 61:1–2 and covenant restoration; Abrahamic covenant; 22:27 (7–38), new covenant; Acts 2:25–36, Davidic covenant; 7:1–53, Abrahamic covenant; 13:47, Isaiah 42:6/49:6 and Isaianic servant covenant; 26:15–18, Isaiah 42:6/49:6 and Isaianic servant covenant.

David, and he will reign over the house of Jacob forever, and of his kingdom there will be no end.

Although the term "covenant" does not appear in the verse there is an allusion to the Davidic covenant (antecedent history) and Christ's rule of God's people (future relationship).

Four of these implicit covenant references are in the infancy narratives. The travel narrative in Luke's Gospel contains five. There are also allusions to the covenant in the preaching of John the Baptist, Jesus' Nazareth sermon, two healing narratives, and two parables. Of the implicit references to the covenant in Acts, five occur in the speeches, whilst the other two are within dialogue.

Evidence of covenant thinking is apparent at an even more implicit level. The covenant blessing of salvation is bestowed upon those who respond to God's unilateral grace by bearing the fruit of repentance, as seen by John the Baptist (Luke 3:2) and the story of Zacchaeus (Luke 19). The forgiveness of sins is associated with covenant blessings dispensed by Jesus, David's heir (Luke 18:38: "He called out, 'Jesus, Son of David, have mercy on me!'").

In writing his portion of salvation history, Luke has adopted a Jewish understanding of the covenant idea, the fluid and comprehensive usage of which results from its definition as a relationship intended to be inviolable, yet one which could be broken, but then again renewed.[68] But then he connects the covenants through Christ: The Abrahamic covenant and the Davidic in the *Benedictus*; the Mosaic covenant and the new covenant in the Lord's Supper; the Abrahamic covenant and the Mosaic in both Peter's and Stephen's speeches.[69]

Each covenant serves a purpose: The universal application of salvation and the expansion of covenant membership to embrace the nations is the main, though not exclusive, purpose of reference to the Abrahamic covenant. The Mosaic covenant is used to point out Israel's unfaithfulness or misunderstanding of it in view of unconditional covenant blessings and to highlight the prospect of the eschatological messianic banquet. The Davidic covenant is significant in that it is used to identify Jesus as the Messiah to dispense the promised salvation. In Luke–Acts, the covenants give the framework for the salvation work of God in Jesus.

---

68. Kovács, "The Covenant Concept as an Organising Principle in Luke–Acts," 146.

69. "The Covenant in Luke–Acts."

3.3.5 Summation

Although salvation is obviously a key theme of Luke–Acts there is a wide diversity of opinion on what Luke is seeking to communicate about this crucial doctrine. Reardon can identify four broad trajectories with respect to Luke's soteriology, with the key issue being the soteriological role of Christ's death. However, when surveying the vast literature on Lukan soteriology he concludes:

> Much of the consternation comes as the result of certain presuppositions about soteriology in general and Luke's apparent inability to satisfy certain soteriological criteria. These presuppositions include preconceptions about the necessary form of atonement (generally expiatory-substitutionary atonement), the assumed priority of Pauline soteriology and an uncritical spiritualization of Lukan soteriological terminology.[70]

The lack of conclusiveness in the atonement debate suggests that it was not the key issue for Luke and it may be better to explore what Luke did seek to emphasize. If we seek to interpret Luke's soteriology on his own terms, through the lens of the OT and as a part of salvation history, two features become prominent: the kingdom of God and the covenants. Luke wanted to demonstrate that salvation comes through entrance into the kingdom of God through the Messiah and that the covenants are a crucial part of God's ancient plan of salvation. In this manner, Luke identified the kingdom of God as a covenant banquet which the Messiah initiates and hosts and into which sinners and tax collectors are invited. Like the kingdom of God, it has a "now" expression, but is yet to be fully consummated.

Whether one identifies the vicarious sacrifice of Christ in Luke–Acts or not, the kingdom of God and the covenants are fundamental elements of Luke's soteriology. Given the OT linkages between καλέω and the covenants, this now creates the space to consider the soteriological use of καλέω by Luke.

3.4 Chapter Summation

The purpose of this chapter was to survey the soteriologies of Luke and Paul and to demonstrate that the focus on justification in the study of Paul's soteriology, and focus on vicarious atonement in the study of Luke's soteriology, has meant that other categories of salvation have been pushed to the

---

70. Reardon, "Recent Trajectories and Themes in Lukan Soteriology," 78.

sidelines. In particular, the covenantal aspects of salvation, with its use of the καλέω language, have not received the attention they deserve.

Even though Luke and Paul use different language when writing about salvation we find here a point of convergence. Both use covenant language in soteriological ways. It is unreasonable to say that this is the "dominant" or even "central" thought in their soteriologies. However, it must be acknowledged that the covenants are a significant part of both writers' understanding of salvation. It is in light of this background that we will turn to Paul and Luke's usage of καλέω language.

4

Paul's Soteriological Use of Call

4.1 Introduction

HAVING REVIEWED THE OT background to the word καλέω and Paul's overall soteriology, attention now turns to Paul's use of καλέω in his Epistles. His writings will be dealt with in a generally agreed chronological order. Fanning's methodology will be used to analyze each usage of the word or its cognates.[1]

Though Paul uses καλέω in about only 22 percent of its NT occurrences, in thirty of these thirty-three uses the action of the verb is performed by a divine agent.[2] In other words, Paul almost always uses καλέω to describe God's activity. With this in mind, we move on to a verse by verse analysis of Paul's usage of καλέω language.

4.2 Galatians 1:6

Upon hearing of reports of false teaching in the Galatian church, and the acceptance of it by some in the church, following the mandatory greetings, Paul moves straight to his issue with the Galatians:

> I am astonished that you are so quickly deserting him who called you (τοῦ καλέσαντος ὑμᾶς) in (ἐν) the grace of Christ and are turning to a different gospel.

There are many metaphors that Paul could have used to describe what the Galatians were doing in "turning to a different gospel." He could have

---

1. Fanning, "Theological Analysis."
2. Klein, "Paul's Use of Kalein: A Proposal," 53.

said they were repudiating their justification by faith, or rejecting their adoption as sons. Given that Paul emphasizes justification by faith so strongly in the Epistle, this would not have been unexpected. However, when Paul sought to describe what it meant when the Galatians were listening to the false teachers and turning away from the gospel, he introduces the language of call.

Paul's use of καλέω language here, and throughout his Epistles, could be interpreted at its most generic level. That is, it could be used in the sense that God had metaphorically called the name of the Galatians believers and that upon hearing his voice they responded and were saved.

However, Paul's use of ἐν suggests that here καλέω has the technical meaning, "to designate as a Christian."[3] Paul is saying, "God named you 'in Christ'" or "God has designated you (to be) 'in Christ.'" The alternative, "God summoned you in (or through) Christ" is also possible but the technical usage is in keeping with Paul's use in Galatians 1:15 and 5:8 (see below).

Further, in describing the situation here, the apostle certainly uses the language of military desertion (v. 6) and political strife (v. 7). But there is also a tragic personal element in the way Paul describes the Galatians' actions.[4] They are in fact abandoning the one who graciously "called" them to himself. It is not merely that they have deserted an idea or a movement. They have deserted the very one who had *saved them at great cost*, not merely *called their name*.

In addition, as we have seen in chapter 2 of this thesis, the word καλέω was loaded with a background and pregnant with meaning for Jews. However, it may also have been a very useful term for Paul's Gentile audience. Chester[5] shows that "called" language was analogous to "conversion" language in antiquity and that in conversion a god called something into existence. The philosopher Epictetus recognized his "call" to his teaching service as a divine act. An awareness of this usage may well be the reason that Paul opts to talk about call when relating to a primarily Gentile audience.

Hence, the "call of God" could well have been a very attractive option for Paul because it had relevance to both his Jewish and Gentile audience. Paul may have used "call" when he spoke to the Galatians about salvation and now that salvation is under threat he refers to it again. In seeking to communicate the gospel to Gentile believers the "once not a people but now called a people" motif associated with call would have been especially appropriate.

3. Ibid., 58.
4. Boice, "Galatians," 428.
5. Chester, *Conversion at Corinth*, 70–77.

The fact that Paul so quickly introduces the terminology of call, even before that of justification, suggests that it was an important part of his soteriology. This is not to suggest that call was a more important image of salvation than justification. It may well have been that call was just an easier image to understand for Gentiles.

4.3 Galatians 1:15

In 1:10–24 Paul is apparently responding to criticism that he is proclaiming his own gospel, not the one from God, and that he is doing so simply to please humans rather than God. In defending himself against these claims, he describes some details related to his conversion:

> But when he who had set me apart before I was born, and who called (καλέσας) me by his grace, was pleased to reveal his Son to (ἐν lit. "in") me, in order that I might preach him among the Gentiles, I did not immediately consult with anyone; nor did I go up to Jerusalem to those who were apostles before me, but I went away into Arabia, and returned again to Damascus.

God did three things for Paul. First, God set him apart from birth. This expression echoes Jeremiah's description of his own calling (Jer 1:5) and may, indeed, consciously reflect it.[6] Second, God called Paul by grace. Paul is using καλέω here as a synonym for salvation. He does not identify what he is called *to*, implying that his readers would know what he meant when he used καλέω without a goal. This is confirmed by 2:8: "For by grace you have been saved through faith." In this later reference to grace he has substituted "called" with "saved," indicating the interchangeability of the terms.

Third, God revealed his Son in Paul (v. 16). The use of ἐν here is difficult to interpret. It may refer to Paul's realization that God had placed the life of the Lord Jesus Christ *in him*. Alternatively, it may refer to the revelation of Jesus Christ through Paul *in others*. It is not possible to reach categorical conclusions. However, the context and the use of ἵνα ("in order that") would suggest that the setting apart, call, and the revelation of God's Son in him was in order that he might become the apostle to the Gentiles. The use of "call," with its vocational flavor, instead of "saved," also supports the notion that the emphasis in this passage is on God's grace in electing Paul to salvation and to the apostleship.

There is no necessary significance in the order of "setting apart," "call," and "revelation" in verse 15. Paul's reversal of these ideas in Romans 1:1

---

6. Boice, "Galatians," 433–4.

("called to be an apostle, set apart for the gospel of God") shows Paul is stressing his apostleship rather making a point about logical or chronological relationships between these terms.[7]

4.4 Galatians 5:8

Paul seeks to highlight the difference between those who desire to add circumcision to Christianity and true believers who trust Christ alone:

> You were running well. Who hindered you from obeying the truth? This persuasion (πεισμονή) is not from him who calls (καλοῦντος) you (Gal 5:7-8).

The technical and soteriological sense of καλοῦντος is implied as no explicit goal is specified. As with Galatians 1:6, Paul describes God as "the one who calls you" rather than "the one who justifies you" or "the one who saves you."

The term πεισμονή is a rare word that appears only here in the NT.[8] It is best to understand it in a pejorative manner as meaning humanly "contrived persuasiveness" in contrast to God's will and purpose. In this sentence, Paul is stating his opinion of the Judaizers: their work and influence have nothing to do with God's will and purpose. This is in contrast to God's call which is consistent.[9] It goes all the way back to his calling the disobedient Adam in the garden (cf. Gen 3:9), and continues with God's call of Abraham, Moses, Samuel, and the prophets, right through to Paul's conveying of the same call to the Galatians. It is a consistent call of salvation, not one that is changed in the way that was being suggested to the Galatians.

4.5 Galatians 5:13

A little further on, Paul tells his readers:

> For you were called (ἐκλήθητε) to freedom, brothers. Only do not use your freedom (τὴν ἐλευθερίαν) as an opportunity for the flesh, but through love serve one another.

The article emphasizes that this is "the" freedom in Christ that Paul has been writing about. The Galatians are not to use this freedom for

---

7. Longenecker, *Galatians*, 41, 30.
8. Ibid., 230-1.
9. Mohrlang and Borchert, *Cornerstone Biblical Commentary*, 314.

immorality. Here, if Galatians is the earliest Epistle we have, is Paul's first written connection between call and ethics. Paul tells his readers that God has called them for the purpose or goal of freedom. But the purpose of the freedom is to love and serve one another. Hence, indirectly, the call of God is a call to ethical living.

Further, the liberation by Christ and God's call are part of the same process of salvation. This is evidenced by Paul using both the aorist (1:6; 5:13) and present tense (5:8) of καλέω in the Epistle. Call is not just the inception of the salvation but an ongoing reality for the Galatians. Call relates not just to salvation but also to sanctification.

4.6 1 Thessalonians 2:11–12

Either just before his Epistle to the Galatians, or shortly after, Paul writes to the Thessalonian church for quite different reasons. There is no threat of false teaching, yet Paul again introduces the language of calling early in the Epistle.

In 1 Thessalonians 2, Paul expands upon what he had said in summary form in 1:5: in Thessalonica Paul and his friends had demonstrated the behaviors of authentic ministers of the gospel. Paul highlights that the manner and content of the missionaries' proclamation also confirmed their authenticity and authority.

> For you know how, like a father with his children, we exhorted each one of you and encouraged you and charged you to walk in a manner worthy of God, who calls (καλοῦντος) you into his own kingdom and glory (vv. 11–12).

The present tense of the participle καλοῦντος ("the one who calls you") suggests the timeless sense of God's call.[10] For Paul, God has always been the covenantal calling God and continues to be so in the present experience of the Thessalonians. As in Galatians 5:8, the present participle indicates that the calling is a dynamic process throughout the life of believers. God continually holds the hope of "kingdom and glory" before them.[11]

Paul refers to the kingdom of God eight times in his Epistles. Here God "calls" the Thessalonians into "his kingdom and glory," alluding to the OT covenants through the term "his kingdom" as well as the term "call" itself.

Paul's references to the kingdom of God typically relate to ethics:

---

10. Bruce, *1 and 2 Thessalonians*, 45, 37.
11. Marshall, "Election and Calling to Salvation in 1 and 2 Thessalonians," 269.

The acts of the flesh are obvious: sexual immorality, impurity and debauchery; idolatry and witchcraft; hatred, discord, jealousy, fits of rage, selfish ambition, dissensions, factions and envy; drunkenness, orgies, and the like. I warn you, as I did before, that those who live like this will not inherit the kingdom of God (Gal 5:19–21).

... nor thieves nor the greedy nor drunkards nor slanderers nor swindlers will inherit the kingdom of God (1 Cor 6:10).

In general, Paul's references to the kingdom are less about grace and more a warning about ethical failing excluding some from the kingdom. But in doing so, they reflect Jesus' emphasis on kingdom ethics as a sign of kingdom membership (e.g. Matt 5:20). These references may reflect Paul's awareness of an oral tradition of Jesus' teaching.

They could also reflect the presence of covenantal nomism in Paul's thinking (see section 3.2). Having been called into salvation through the new covenant, holiness is an essential sign of belonging, just as it was for those who had been saved by membership of the OT covenants. Covenant call imagery is not a peripheral element of Pauline soteriology but a primary motivator for correct conduct.

As with the Galatian Epistle, Paul could have used any one of a range of soteriological metaphors here, but he chooses the language of calling. Indeed, he uses calling in 1 Thessalonians when he does not mention justification or adoption.

4.7 1 Thessalonians 4:7

In the main body of 1 Thessalonians Paul gives instructions on pleasing God (4:1–12), the second coming (4:13—5:11), community conduct (5:12–22), and prayer and assurance (5:23–24). In 4:3–8 he focuses on sexual holiness. Some Gentile converts may have found it a struggle to adjust to a new ethical code. But Paul argues in verse 7:

For God has not called (ἐκάλεσεν) us for (ἐπί) impurity, but in (ἐν) holiness.

The change of preposition from ἐπί to ἐν in the second part of the sentence implies that sanctification is part of the Christian calling rather than just the outcome.[12] By calling his people God saves them in the sense of setting them apart for himself. Certainly, ἐν can also be translated as "into,"

12. Bruce, *1 and 2 Thessalonians*, 85–86.

implying that holiness is the consequence of the calling. However, it is within the range of meaning of the text to imply that call and sanctification are intimately and soteriologically linked.

4.8 1 Thessalonians 5:24

In the concluding exhortations, Paul writes (5:23–24):

> Now may the God of peace himself sanctify you completely, and may your whole spirit and soul and body be kept blameless at the coming of our Lord Jesus Christ. He who calls (καλῶν) you is faithful; he will surely do it.

This is another instance where Paul uses call language in a technical way. The ones who are "kept blameless" are surely the saved, here designated simply as "the called." What the readers are called from or to is not identified, yet Paul considers the meaning is still clear.

The verb is a present active participle. Apparently, Westcott, referring to this verse, said to a friend, "I think there is meaning in that present participle."[13] It is God who calls his people to sanctification (cf. 1 Pet 1:15: "As he who called you is holy, you also be holy in your conduct") and he supplies the grace without which his call cannot be realized.

There is also an echo of covenant here. YHWH is "faithful," a word often associated with covenant (cf. Deut 7:9; Isa 49:7; 1 Cor 1:9; 10:13; 2 Cor 1:18; 2 Thess 3:3), giving Paul's readers confidence in his established, settled, unchanging character. It is a reminder of the trustworthy God who initiates and perfects (cf. Phil 1:6; 2:13).

4.9 2 Thessalonians 1:11

If Pauline authorship is accepted, and efforts to prove 2 Thessalonians was written before 1 Thessalonians fail, a date shortly after 1 Thessalonians is most probable for the writing of 2 Thessalonians.[14] Following the usual greetings, verses 3–10 describe Paul's confidence in the believers and in God's judgment on the unbelievers. Verses 11–12 are a summary of verses 3–10:

> To this end we always pray for you, that our God may make you worthy (ἀξιώσῃ) of his calling (κλήσεως) and may fulfil every

---

13. Ibid., 131.
14. Thomas, "2 Thessalonians," 303.

resolve for good and every work of faith by his power so that the name of our Lord Jesus may be glorified in you, and you in him, according to the grace of our God and the Lord Jesus Christ.

The prayer "that our God may count you worthy of his calling" probably relates to their worthiness for the kingdom mentioned in verse 5: "This is evidence of the righteous judgment of God, that you may be considered worthy (καταξιωθῆναι from the root ἄξιος) of the kingdom of God, for which you are also suffering." Having declared that the Thessalonian Christians will be considered *worthy* of the kingdom, Paul's prayer for them is that they may be made *worthy* of this calling. As in 1 Thessalonians 2:12, the writer has linked belonging to the kingdom of God and calling, in this case through the term "worthy."

4.10 2 Thessalonians 2:14

In 2:3–12 the writer insists that the Thessalonians can know that the day of the Lord has not come. Verses 13ff. are in contrast to the doom of the unbelievers described in verses 11–12. The writer reassures the Thessalonians that they were elected by God to be saved when Jesus returns:

> But we ought always to give thanks to God for you, brothers beloved by the Lord, because God chose you as the firstfruits to be saved, through sanctification by the Spirit and belief in the truth. To this he called (ἐκάλεσεν) you through our gospel, so that you may obtain the glory of our Lord Jesus Christ.

The author puts his reassurance in the form of a prayer-report. Any uncertainty about the reader's destiny should be overcome by a recollection of their Christian status.[15] God chose them as firstfruits to be saved. He has "called" them to "this" (v. 14)—their salvation through sanctification by the Spirit and belief in the truth—through the preaching of the gospel (cf. 1 Thess 1:4–5; Gal 1:6–7). The call is both a present experience and a future hope ("the glory of Christ" v. 14).

Although the writer uses εἵλατο (from αιρεω "to take or pick"; used only here and in Phil 1:22) rather than ἐξελέξατο, election is still clearly in focus. The call-election-salvation relationship is again in evidence.

---

15. Marshall, "2 Thessalonians," 1289.

4.11 1 Corinthians 1:2

Characteristically, Paul begins the Epistle by naming himself and also by identifying his position as an apostle of Jesus Christ:

> Paul, called (κλητός) by the will of God to be an apostle of Christ Jesus, and our brother Sosthenes, To the church (ἐκκλησίᾳ) of God that is in Corinth, to those sanctified in Christ Jesus, called (κλητοῖς) to be saints together with all those who in every place call upon (ἐπικαλουμένοις) the name of our Lord Jesus Christ, both their Lord and ours: Grace to you and peace from God our Father and the Lord Jesus Christ.

If one counts, ἐκκλησία, καλέω, and its cognates appear four times in his opening two verses. Just as in his correspondence to the Galatians and Thessalonians, Paul introduces the language of call early in his Epistle to the Corinthians. He does not mention justification until later (1 Cor 6:11).

At the beginning point of his letter Paul wants to affirm the identity of his readers. Just as he became an apostle because of God's call, his readers are God's holy people by virtue of God's call. Further, just as Paul's call to be an apostle was the historical expression of the prior will of God, so was that of the Corinthians. The believers in Corinth are also designated as the "church of God," a phrase that has OT associations, as in the expression "assembly (or congregation) of the Lord" (Num 16:3; 20:4; Deut 23:1; 1 Chr 28:8) and the "assembly of Israel" (Lev 16:17; Deut 31:30). Paul is implying that the Corinthian church has a similar relationship to God as the nation of Israel. The OT references to the "assembly of the Lord/Israel" also have covenantal overtones (esp. 1 Chr 28:8), making his use of call language especially appropriate.

The ancient Greek ἐκκλησία (assemblies) were gatherings of the citizenry in a city-state to discuss and decide on matters of public interest (cf. Acts 19:39; Herodotus, *Histories*, 3.142), as they certainly did in Corinth itself according to ancient inscriptions found there.[16] Vine[17] boldly declares that:

> The term *ekklēsia* is from *ek*, "out of" and *klesis*, "a calling" (*kaleo*—"to call").

One must be careful to avoid placing too much authority in meaning derived from etymology because meaning changes over time (for example,

---

16. Mare, "1 Corinthians," 188.
17. Vine, *Vine's Complete Expository Dictionary of Old and New Testament Words*, 42.

the English word cupboard). However, given that ἐκκλησία is originally derived from κλῆσις, one should not rule out the possibility that Paul is deliberately using ἐκκλησία and κλῆσις in close proximity. It is quite plausible that Paul was implying that the ἐκκλησία τοῦ θεοῦ is composed of the "called out" ones.

Paul then designates his readers as those sanctified in Jesus Christ (v. 2). But they are also the κλητοῖς ἁγίοις—the called saints. The structure suggests that the two are related, if not synonymous. Once again, that call is not just to salvation but also to sanctification.

4.12 1 Corinthians 1:9

Before concluding his opening thanksgiving, Paul assures the Corinthians of God's faithfulness:

> God is faithful, by whom you were called (ἐκλήθητε) into the fellowship of his Son, Jesus Christ our Lord.

As we have seen, the term "God is faithful" would have been loaded with covenantal implications. It would not be surprising to any Jewish readers that Paul would also refer to their calling in close proximity. Given the heavy emphasis on election in this chapter (in vv. 9, 24, 26, 27, 28), it is not surprising that calling and covenant would also feature heavily.

By using the aorist tense Paul implies that God called the Corinthians into fellowship with Jesus Christ at salvation. The ongoing result of God's call is κοινωνία with Christ. Keener[18] points out that ancient philosophers often spoke of human "fellowship" with other people. Although Paul could be referring to fellowship with others in Christ, he could also mean something far more unusual in antiquity: intimacy with God. Greco-Roman religion tended to stress ritual (or, in some cults, non-relational ecstasy). Judaism viewed God as intimate with his people, but it did not claim to experience the intimacy implied here by Paul.

However, Paul is also advocating Christian community in this passage. "The sense would be that God has called you into the community—that is, the church, of Jesus Christ."[19] One cannot enjoy fellowship with Christ while being at odds with other members of his body (see 1 Cor 12).[20] Paul makes a transition from what God had done in the past in saving them, and will do in the future, in sanctifying them, to what the Corinthians needed to

18. Keener, *The IVP Bible Background Commentary: New Testament*.
19. Barrett, *A Commentary on the Epistle to the Romans*, 40.
20. Lowery, "1 Corinthians," 508.

do in the present, namely, mend their divisions. Their call includes the call to fellowship in Christ and its related call to Christian community, whether the Corinthians liked it or not.

4.13 1 Corinthians 1:26

In verses 1:17b–4:21 Paul is trying to demonstrate that the divisions in the Corinthian church can be healed if the Corinthians see the distinction between the world's wisdom and God's wisdom. Having contrasted God's strength and human weakness, he now speaks about the circumstances of his readers when they were called. In 1:26–29 he writes:

> For consider your calling (κλῆσιν), brothers: not many of you were wise according to worldly standards, not many were powerful, not many were of noble birth. But God chose (ἐξελέξατο) the foolish things of the world to shame the wise; God chose the weak things of the world to shame the strong. God chose the lowly things of this world and the despised things—and the things that are not—to nullify the things that are, so that no one may boast before him.

The calling (κλῆσιν) Paul asks his readers to consider could be their vocation or status before they were saved (not wise, powerful, or of noble birth). However, most scholars recognize "your calling" as a reference to conversion not vocation.[21] This is affirmed by the connection between call and election in the passage. In verses 27–28, Paul says God chose (ἐξελέξατο) the weak, despised, and lowly. The "things that were not" were excluded, but God demonstrated his refusal to accept this by granting them existence on his higher authority. God's calling brings things into existence that previously did not exist.[22] This eccentric calling reflects the rationale of God's call of Israel:

> For you are a people holy to the LORD your God. The LORD your God has chosen you out of all the peoples on the face of the earth to be his people, his treasured possession. The LORD did not set his affection on you and choose you because you were more numerous than other peoples, for you were the fewest of all peoples. But it was because the LORD loved you and kept the oath he swore to your ancestors that he brought you out with a

---

21. Morris, *The First Epistle of Paul to the Corinthians: An Introduction and Commentary*, 7, 47; Marsh, "1 Corinthians," 1352; Mare, "1 Corinthians," 195.

22. Chester, *Conversion at Corinth*, 79.

mighty hand and redeemed you from the land of slavery, from the power of Pharaoh king of Egypt (Deut 7:6–8).

Just as there was no apparent logic for the selection of Israel to be the Lord's chosen people, there was no human logic in God's choice of those at Corinth who would be saved. The close association here suggests that "in Paul's parlance, calling is a synonym for divine election."[23]

4.14 1 Corinthians 7:15–24

After addressing the problems reported by the people of Chloe's household (1:11), Paul began to answer the questions that had been sent to him (7:1—14:40). The Corinthians had asked at least two questions concerning marriage. The first was whether a Christian should get married at all (7:1), and the second was whether virgins should get married (7:25).[24]

> But if the unbelieving partner separates, let it be so. In such cases the brother or sister is not enslaved. God has called (κέκληκεν) you to peace. For how do you know, wife, whether you will save your husband? Or how do you know, husband, whether you will save your wife? Only let each person lead the life that the Lord has assigned to him, and to which God has called (κέκληκεν) him. This is my rule in all the churches. Was anyone at the time of his call (ἐκλήθη) already circumcised? Let him not seek to remove the marks of circumcision. Was anyone at the time of his call (κέκληταί) uncircumcised? Let him not seek circumcision. For neither circumcision counts for anything nor uncircumcision, but keeping the commandments of God. Each one should remain in the condition in which he was called (ἐκλήθη). Were you a bondservant when called (ἐκλήθης)? Do not be concerned about it. (But if you can gain your freedom, avail yourself of the opportunity.) For he who was called (κληθείς) in the Lord as a bondservant is a freedman of the Lord. Likewise he who was free when called (κληθείς) is a bondservant of Christ. You were bought with a price; do not become bondservants of men. So, brothers, in whatever condition each was called (ἐκλήθη), there let him remain with God.

Here is another instance of Paul using καλέω as a technical term. He could merely say, "You were called," and, omitting any instrument or goal, be confident that his readers would understand just what he was meaning.

23. Ciampa and Rosner, *The First Letter to the Corinthians*, 103.
24. Mare, "1 Corinthians," 227.

They knew that through his use of καλέω Paul meant to say "called to become a believer."[25]

In applying the principle that God has called his people to live in peace (v. 15), Paul teaches that believers should live (lit. "continue to walk") with contentment in whatever situation of life God places them. In each case he presents for consideration, God is the one who calls. The perfect tense form κέκληκεν ("God has called") in verse 15 stresses the initial divine call of the believer with its continuing sense of status.

God calls people to salvation while they are situated in a calling or circumstance (married, unmarried, circumcised, uncircumcised, slave, or free). He calls people to be "in Christ" (1:9), but the call comes in a given socioeconomic setting. God's call in Christ renders those settings irrelevant (7:24). Because of this, one may live out the Christian life in whatever setting the call took place. If a change of situation does take place, that too is irrelevant. The call *to* Christ has created such a change in one's relationship with God that one does not need to seek to change other relationships. The latter relationships are transformed and given new meaning by the former.[26]

And so, Paul's usage of call here broadens its meaning from just the call to salvation to God's call to a situation in life. "Let each person lead the life that the Lord has assigned to him, and to which God has called (κέκληκεν) him" (v. 17). Paul is not just talking soteriologically but also vocationally. This fact, that God had called each one to a vocation, and seeks from each one faithful service in that calling, elevates and sanctifies both the work and the worker.[27] As a result, the call of God means that believers can "live in peace" (v. 15).

The calling is primarily addressed to individuals (note the singular throughout this section) and not to existing groups or communities.[28] Paul has individualized calling. In this passage he has also personalized it. In 7:21 he asks, "Were you a slave when you were called?" Such a question suggests individuals should look back and identify their own circumstances when they were called. This type of question would normally have been nonsensical for a Jewish reader since it was the nation to which they belong which had been called. But ethnic distinctions are now irrelevant to a person's standing before God. There is nothing to be gained by changing one's ethnic status, and Paul opposed the Judaizers when they attempted to promote it.

---

25. Klein, "Paul's Use of Kalein: A Proposal," 59-60.

26. Moo, *The New International Commentary on the New Testament: The Epistle to the Romans*, 307.

27. Lowery, "1 Corinthians," 519.

28. Chester, *Conversion at Corinth*, 107-8.

Similarly, social status is irrelevant to one's status before God. An advance in status should not be sought, but may be accepted.

4.15 Romans 1:6-7

Again, right at the beginning of his correspondence to the Romans, Paul introduces a concept which will be a major one through the Epistle—the call of God:

> Paul, a servant of Christ Jesus, called (κλητός) to be an apostle, set apart for the gospel of God, which he promised beforehand through his prophets in the holy Scriptures, concerning his Son, who was descended from David according to the flesh and was declared to be the Son of God in power according to the Spirit of holiness by his resurrection from the dead, Jesus Christ our Lord, through whom we have received grace and apostleship to bring about the obedience of faith for the sake of his name among all the nations, including you who are called (κλητοί) to belong to Jesus Christ (κλητοὶ Ἰησοῦ Χριστοῦ). To all those in Rome who are loved by God and called to be saints (κλητοῖς ἁγίοις): Grace to you and peace from God our Father and the Lord Jesus Christ.

In this greeting Paul is seeking to clarify his apostolic relationship with the Romans. His calling is to bring about faithful obedience amongst the nations (v. 5), including those described as "called" (κλητοί). Paul's readers were not called, as he was, to apostleship, but were called "to belong to Jesus Christ" and to be "saints," the common term designating believers.[29]

The κλητοὶ Ἰησοῦ Χριστοῦ (lit. "the called of Jesus Christ") is best translated "who are called to belong to Jesus Christ." It is God the Father who calls (8:30), not Jesus. When God issues his call, he claims his loved ones as Christ's possession. Like God's people in the OT they have been set inside the intimate circle of God's love.[30] This almost forceful taking of possession echoes Isaiah 43:1:

> But now thus says the LORD,
>   he who created you, O Jacob,
>   he who formed you, O Israel:
> "Fear not, for I have redeemed you;
>   I have called you by name (LXX: ἐκάλεσά σε τὸ ὄνομά), you are mine.

---

29. Harrison, "Romans," 15.
30. Allen, "Romans," 1317.

But not only are the Romans called to belong to Jesus Christ, they are called to be saints (κλητοῖς ἁγίοις). This term has its origin in OT descriptions of Israel as "a holy nation" or "holy people."[31] It echoes a term used of Israel—"sacred assembly" (LXX: κλητὴ ἁγία in Exod 12:16; Lev 23; Num 28:25). It was later used more narrowly to describe the elect in Israel who would share in the blessings of the messianic kingdom.

Such language reminds the recipients that they too are God's people, whether Jew or Gentile. Although the term "covenant" is not used in this passage, the language of God's "loved" and "called out" people is covenantal. Paul would go on to use other soteriological terms in the book of Romans, but here at the beginning, where he is seeking to define himself and the community of Roman believers to which he writes, call language is best suited for his purposes.

It should also be noted that Paul's usage of "saints" was always plural (except in Phil 4:21).[32] As indicated in 1 Corinthians, being called to be a saint is a corporate matter. To be a Christian is to be part of a community, a family, or a body.

4.16 Romans 4:16–17

In Romans 4:1–25, Paul presents Abraham as a test case for the view that justification is by faith alone. Abraham was the father of the Jewish people, and hence his example is crucial for Paul's argument.[33]

> Therefore, the promise comes by faith, so that it may be by grace and may be guaranteed to all Abraham's offspring—not only to those who are of the law but also to those who have the faith of Abraham. He is the father of us all. As it is written: "I have made you a father of many nations." He is our father in the sight of God, in whom he believed—the God who gives life to the dead and calls (καλοῦντος) into being things that were not (Rom 4:16–17).

"Gives life to the dead" and "calling into existence" are a reference to the birth of Isaac from Abraham's "dead" body and Sarah's "dead" womb when both were far beyond the age of childbearing (v. 19). However, the idea of "calling into existence" also echoes God's creative activity. Like Isaiah (42:5–9; 43:8–21; 45:1–7; 48:6–11; also Ps 33:6), Paul understands "calling"

---

31. Peterson, "Holiness," 548.
32. Utley, "Romans 1:7."
33. Dennis and Grudem, *The ESV Study Bible*, 2164.

as the creative and life-giving act of God. This is further evidence that for Paul "call" is not just a historical event but the creation of a new identity with new goals, ethics, and purposes.[34] Given this understanding of calling as creation, it is not surprising that Paul rarely discusses a human response. God calls and God sanctifies. His vocabulary of calling is used again to denote the divine dimension of conversion.

4.17 Romans 8:28–30

One of Paul's important usages of call is in this famous passage. He began a major section of the Epistle (5:1—8:39) by emphasizing the final hope of believers (5:1—11). Now he concludes with the same emphasis. In a section where Paul is contrasting the present suffering with the future glory, he refers to God's call three times—once in verse 28 and twice in verse 30:

> And we know that for those who love God all things work together for good, for those who are called (κλητοῖς) according to his purpose. For those whom he foreknew he also predestined to be conformed to the image of his Son, in order that he might be the firstborn among many brothers. And those whom he predestined he also called (ἐκάλεσεν), and those whom he called (ἐκάλεσεν) he also justified, and those whom he justified he also glorified.

"Those who love God" (v. 28) is an OT expression for those who throw themselves wholeheartedly into God's service and identify themselves with his aims. Its use is evident in the covenant context of Exodus 20:5-6:

> You shall not bow down to them or serve them, for I the LORD your God am a jealous God, visiting the iniquity of the fathers on the children to the third and the fourth generation of those who hate me, but showing steadfast love to thousands of *those who love me* and keep my commandments.[35]

Paul uses the term "those who love God" in parallel with "those who are called (κλητοῖς οὖσιν) according to his purpose." In doing so he indicates that "the called" are the ones who love God, that is, those enjoying a covenantal salvation.

To explain the statement in verse 28, Paul goes on in verse 29 to give an explanation of how it is that those who love him and are called by him find

---

34. Chester, *Conversion at Corinth*, 105-6.
35. See also Judg 5:31; Dan 9:4.

that all things work for good. First, God foreknows (προώρισεν) those he has predestined. This may mean what it often does in Greek literature—"know something ahead of time."[36] But Paul says that it is "the called" whom God knows, and this suggests the more personal idea of "knowing" that is sometimes found in the OT: election into personal relationship (e.g. Gen 18:19; Jer 1:5; Amos 3:2). To "know" refers to God's covenantal love in which he sets his affection on those he has chosen. This is almost certainly the sense that "foreknow" has in its other NT occurrences (11:2; Acts 2:23; 1 Pet 1:2, 20).

God's foreknowing leads to his "predestining them"—his appointing them to a specific destiny. This destiny is that they become like Christ, the final event that God accomplishes by "calling," "justifying," and "glorifying." All the verbs in 8:30 are in the aorist tense, suggesting that, though the attaining of glory may be future, it is already accomplished because God determines it.

Some have boldly drawn significant conclusions from the order of the verbs in this passage. Klein[37] says that since in Paul's list of God's actions "calling" follows the pretemporal (before the beginning of time) actions of "foreknow" and "predestine," it marks the point of reception of salvation for those embraced in the previous two actions. Those called are then justified and glorified, the final two actions.

Similarly, Wright can conclude:

> The point is that the word "justification" does not itself denote the process whereby, or the event in which, a person is brought by grace from unbelief, idolatry and sin into faith, true worship and renewal of life. Paul, clearly and unambiguously, uses a different word for that, the word "call." The word "justification," despite centuries of Christian misuse, is used by Paul to denote that which happens immediately after the "call": "those God called, he also justified" (Romans 8:30).[38]

However, too much can be made of the order of the terms that Paul uses here. The fact that call seems to come before foreknowledge in verse 28, but then proceeds from predestination in verse 30, would serve to warn those who are seeking to identify some sort of chronological sequence in the salvation process from these verses. Suffice to say that call, foreknowledge, predestination, justification, and glorification are all part of the phenomenon of salvation. Although the exact order in which they occur is complex, their importance is shared.

36. Schreiner, *Romans*, 452.
37. Klein, *The New Chosen People: A Corporate View of Election*, 202.
38. Wright, *Paul: In Fresh Perspective*, 121–2.

What can also be concluded is that God's promises cannot fail because they are based on his call. God's unstoppable plan cannot be thwarted and he uses all things to bring about the fulfillment of his purposes.[39] Dunn says the οὖσιν in τοῖς οὖσιν κλητοῖς ("those who are called") should be understood in a "pregnant" sense: they are called and stand now in, and under, this call which has opened, and continues to open, them to God's encouragement.[40] "Calling is the realization in history of God's eternal purpose. It is here, in God's purpose, that the ultimate assurance of salvation rests."[41]

4.18 Romans 9:7

English translations tend to use words like "reckoned" (NIV) or "named" (ESV) when translating καλέω in Romans 9:7. The context of these verses is Paul's discussion of God's choice of both Israel and the Gentiles. Paul's argument is that God's choice is sovereign, not based on ancestry or works:

> But it is not as though the word of God has failed. For not all who are descended from Israel belong to Israel, and not all are children of Abraham because they are his offspring, but "Through Isaac shall your offspring be named (κληθήσεται)."

Although this passage does not explicitly use the call of God in relation to believers, κληθήσεταί is clearly used in a soteriological sense. The quotes in verse 7 pick up the LXX translation of Genesis 21:12: ὅτι ἐν Ἰσαακ κληθήσεταί σοι σπέρμα ("for in Isaac shall your seed be called") with its covenantal and hence soteriological flavor.

Paul concludes that the failure of the Jews to respond to the gospel of Christ does not mean God's word had failed. There had never been a promise that every Jewish person would be saved. Instead, this rejection, and the choice of the Gentiles, is simply the current example of the principle of God's sovereign choice established in the OT.[42] Hence, Paul frequently talks about the call of God in this section on Israel. Indeed, Dunn calls the section 9:6–29 "The Call of God."[43] It is the overarching soteriological term into which other concepts, such as election, fit.

---

39. Klein, *The New Chosen People: A Corporate View of Election*, 201.
40. Dunn, *Romans 1–8*, 38a, 482.
41. Barrett, *A Commentary on the Epistle to the Romans*, 169.
42. Witmer, "Romans 9:6–9."
43. Dunn, *Romans 9–16*, 38b, 536.

4.19 Romans 9:10–13

Paul further illustrates his point by reference to Jacob and Esau:

> And not only so, but also when Rebekah had conceived children by one man, our forefather Isaac, though they were not yet born and had done nothing either good or bad—in order that God's purpose of election might continue, not because of works but because of him who calls (καλοῦντος)—she was told, "The older will serve the younger." As it is written, "Jacob I loved, but Esau I hated."

Esau and Jacob are evidence that God did not promise that every person of Jewish descent would be saved, for they were both from the chosen line, yet God chose Jacob and not Esau. God chose Jacob to achieve his purpose of election (v. 11) and not because of Jacob's works, "but because of him who calls." It is the "calling" character of God that saves, not good works.

Paul is using call here as a substitute for other soteriological terms because of its close relationship with covenant and election. Although the term covenant is not used, it is clearly in focus. "It is the call of God which makes, maintains and characterizes the covenant."[44] For Paul, gospel and covenant choice, promise and call are a tightly bound package. It is the continuity of God's call and promise across the covenants which led Paul to assert that those who insist on works of law are denying not only the gospel but their own election. Repeatedly throughout the letter Paul has taught, both implicitly and explicitly, that the gospel he proclaims to Gentiles is the fulfillment of God's covenant promise to Israel.[45]

4.20 Romans 9:22–26

As Paul continues to discuss God's sovereign choice he asks:

> What if God, desiring to show his wrath and to make known his power, has endured with much patience vessels of wrath

---

44. Ibid., 549.
45. Ibid., 536.

prepared for destruction, in order to make known the riches of his glory for vessels of mercy, which he has prepared beforehand for glory—even us whom he has called (ἐκάλεσεν), not from the Jews only but also from the Gentiles? As indeed he says in Hosea,
"Those who were not my people I will call (καλέσω) 'my people,' and he who was not beloved I will call 'beloved.'"
"And in the very place where it was said to them,
'You are not my people,' there they will be called (κληθήσονται) 'sons of the living God.'"

In 9:7–13 Paul had shown how God called from within ethnic Israel a smaller number of Jews who formed a "spiritual" Israel. Now he shows that this sovereign call of God has in the present time created a new people, composed of both Gentiles (vv. 25–26) and a Jewish remnant (vv. 27–29).

In 9:25 Paul quotes from Hosea 2:23, which actually refers to the change in Israel's status from being called "not my people" to being "my people." However, in both Romans 9:25 and 1 Peter 2:10 the application is broadened to include non-Jews. Gentiles, who are not actually a people, but only masses of humanity, are called by the grace of God to be the people of God.

The phrase "my people" is an expression of endearment. It appears seventeen times in the book of Exodus alone (for example, Exod 6:7: "I will take you to be my people, and I will be your God, and you shall know that I am the LORD your God, who has brought you out from under the burdens of the Egyptians"). The last clause of Hosea 1:9 ("I am not your God") is literally, "and I [am] not I AM (*'ehyeh*) to you." The statement probably alludes to God's words to Moses, "I am (*'ehyeh*) who I am (*'ehyeh*). This is what you are to say to the Israelites: I AM (*'ehyeh*) has sent me to you" (Exod 3:14). "I AM," which is closely related to the divine name YHWH, points to God as the covenant LORD of Israel who watches over and delivers his people (cf. Exod 3:16–17). However, through the naming of Lo-Ammi, YHWH announced that Israel would no longer experience his special saving presence.[46] The term "not my people" would have cut to the heart of Israel's self-understanding as the elect, covenantal people of God. With these covenantal themes in mind Paul's use of "call" language is quite understandable.

Although Paul's use of the Hosea passages basically follows the text of the LXX, he alters the verb ἐρῶ ("I will say") in Hosea 2:23 to καλέσω ("I will call") in Romans 9:25. This substitution is noteworthy. For Paul, καλέσω was a better description of God's intended, and now completed, actions

---

46. Robert B. Chisholm Jr., "Hosea," 1381.

towards the Gentiles than ἐρῶ. It again emphasizes how useful call was to Paul's soteriology.

He uses "call" again in 9:26 (quoting Hosea 1:10): "Where it was said to them, 'You are not my people,' there they will be called (κληθήσονται) 'sons of the living God.'" The term, "sons of the living God" points to the restoration of the covenant relationship, using the imagery of a family (cf. 2:1–5). Paul finds an opening in this new name for God's people to include the Gentiles. No longer will God's people be called simply, "My people." Now they will be called by an inclusive name—"sons of the living God."

As Klein concludes: "Paul's use of *kalein* in Rom 9:25 implies God's causative, effectual action in bringing a people from the condition 'not his people' to the condition 'his people.'"[47]

4.21 Romans 11:28–29

In summarizing the argument of chapters 9–11, Paul, referring to Israel says:

> As regards the gospel, they are enemies for your sake. But as regards election (ἐκλογὴν), they are beloved for the sake of their forefathers. For the gifts and the calling (κλῆσις) of God are irrevocable. For just as you were at one time disobedient to God but now have received mercy because of their disobedience, so they too have now been disobedient in order that by the mercy shown to you they also may now receive mercy. For God has consigned all to disobedience, that he may have mercy on all (Rom 11:28–32).

Verses 28–32 are formulated with particular care as revealed by the rhetorical structure. The structure means that they provide a fitting summary and climax of the preceding argument.[48] The use of election (ἐκλογὴν), calling (κλῆσις), and mercy (ἠλεήθητε) gather together the key elements and main thrust of Romans 9–11.

Verse 29 is literally, "irrevocable are the gifts and the calling of God" (ἀμεταμέλητα γὰρ τὰ χαρίσματα καὶ ἡ κλῆσις τοῦ θεοῦ.) The word translated "irrevocable" is given the place of emphasis at the beginning of the sentence. The gifts of God are the special privileges of Israel mentioned in 9:4–5:

> Theirs is the adoption to sonship; theirs the divine glory, the covenants, the receiving of the law, the temple worship and the promises. Theirs are the patriarchs, and from them is traced the

---

47. Klein, "Paul's Use of Kalein: A Proposal," 55.
48. Dunn, *Romans 9–16*, 38b, 677.

human ancestry of the Messiah, who is God over all, forever praised!

The phrase χαρίσματα καὶ κλῆσις ("gifts and calling") can be understood variously:[49]

1. As two distinct categories (Cranfield);
2. With κλῆσις (calling) as the particular and most important of these χαρίσματα (gifts) (Michel);
3. As a hendiadys (the expression of an idea by the use of usually two independent words connected by "and") (Käsemann).

Whichever way, calling is clearly an integral part of God's salvation purposes for Israel and now for the followers of the Messiah. Calling, election, adoption, glory, the covenants, the law, the temple, the patriarchs, and the Messiah are all interrelated parts of God's great salvation purposes for the world.

4.22 Ephesians 1:18

The Christian blessing in verses 3–14 has "intervened" between the opening salutation and the thanksgiving that normally follows it in Paul's letters.[50] The writer's thanksgiving for the spiritual progress of the audience arises out of what he has just written in verses 13 and 14. He is praying that his readers may be fully endowed with the Holy Spirit and with his spiritual powers of wisdom and revelation:

> I do not cease to give thanks for you, remembering you in my prayers, that the God of our Lord Jesus Christ, the Father of glory, may give you the Spirit of wisdom and of revelation in the knowledge of him, having the eyes of your hearts enlightened, that you may know what is the hope to which he has called you (ἐλπὶς τῆς κλήσεως αὐτοῦ; lit. "the hope of his calling"), what are the riches of his glorious inheritance in the saints . . .

The OT also spoke of opening one's eyes to God's word (Ps 119:18) or to other spiritual realities (2 Kgs 6:17). Jewish people commonly prayed for enlightened eyes to understand God's word.[51] The writer's prayer in Ephesians is a petition for a threefold enlightenment. The three clauses beginning

---

49. Ibid., 686.
50. Wood, "Ephesians," 29.
51. Keener, *The IVP Bible Background Commentary: New Testament.*

with "what" (τίς, τίς, and τί) that the author asks for are: (1) knowledge of the hope God's calling brings, (2) knowledge of the wealth of glory laid up in his inheritance in the saints, and (3) knowledge of the immensity of his power.[52] The first enlightenment prayed for, knowledge of hope, looks to the future. That which believers hope for, the "glorious inheritance," is clearly the consummation of their salvation. But the believer's hope has its source in their earlier calling (κλήσεως).

As in Galatians, 1 Corinthians, and Romans, Paul (or the one writing in his name) has quickly introduced the language of call and used it soteriologically. Further, he has used κλήσεως in a place where it could easily have said ". . . that you may know what is the hope of his salvation" or ". . . the hope of his justification." Again, we cannot be categorical about the reasons κλήσεως is used here, but its usage is suggestive of the importance of call in Pauline soteriology.

4.23 Ephesians 4:1, 4

At this point the Epistle turns to exhortation based upon the principles presented in the first three chapters. There are three subsections in chapter 4: verses 1–6, 7–10 and 11–16. The first section, 4:1–6, is an exhortation to unity:

> I therefore, a prisoner for the Lord, urge (Παρακαλῶ) you to walk in a manner worthy (ἀξίως) of the calling (κλήσεως) to which you have been called (ἐκλήθητε), with all humility and gentleness, with patience, bearing with one another in love, eager to maintain the unity of the Spirit in the bond of peace. There is one body and one Spirit—just as you were called (ἐκλήθητε) to the one hope that belongs to your call (κλήσεως)—one Lord, one faith, one baptism, one God and Father of all, who is over all and through all and in all.

Suggestively, the writer uses wordplay between three words that share the same καλέω root: "I . . . urge (Παρακαλῶ) . . . calling (κλήσεως) . . . you have been called (ἐκλήθητε)." καλέω is also etymologically related to the term (ἐκκλησίᾳ) "church" used in the previous verse (3:21). It would appear that the writer is deliberately drawing attention to the centrality of καλέω.

The word translated "worthy" (v. 1) (ἀξίως) suggests a comparison of two things, like a weighing on a scale. Thus, to live a life worthy of our

---

52. Lincoln, *Ephesians*, 42, 58.

calling is to live in a way "comparable," or "suitable" to God's calling.[53] There are four qualities which reflect a life worthy of one's calling (v. 2): humility, gentleness, patience, and love. The absence of these qualities would jeopardize Christian unity. Hence, in this passage, the calling refers not only to believers' salvation but also to a unity in the one body. The Christian's call influences not only their personal life but their relationship to other believers in the body.[54]

The "divine passive" nature of the verb in verse 1 underlines what is already inherent in the idea of the call: God's initiative in bringing humanity to the goal for which he intended it. The appeal to live worthily of God's calling presupposes that God's gracious initiative requires a continuous human response and that his call bestows both high privilege and high responsibility.[55] In exhorting to a way of life that corresponds to such a calling, the writer sought to ensure that what followed was not to be seen as mere moral advice but as a fitting response to the soteriological call.

The usage of call in this passage is similar to that found in the undisputed Pauline Epistles, where call brings ethical responsibilities, especially through the notion of living a corporate life "worthy" of the call. What is unique to its usage in Ephesians is its linkage of call to hope.

4.24 Colossians 3:15

The beginning of chapter 3 marks the end to the author's polemic against false teaching and is a bridge to his appeals for the Colossians to live in a manner pleasing to the Lord. In 3:12–17 he calls the Colossians to a holy lifestyle, consistent with their new identity. In verses 14–15 he writes:

> And above all these put on love, which binds everything together in perfect harmony. And let the peace of Christ rule in your hearts, to which indeed you were called (ἐκλήθητε) in one body.

There are three ways the NT speaks of peace:[56] (1) as the objective (doctrinal) aspect of our peace with God through Christ (Rom 5:1); (2) as the subjective (experiential) aspect of our being right with God (John 14:27; 16:33; Phil 4:7); and (3) as God's uniting of Jews and Gentiles into one new

---

53. Hoehner, Comfort, and Davids, *Cornerstone Biblical Commentary: Ephesians, Philippians, Colossians, 1 & 2 Thessalonians, Philemon*, 16, 78.

54. Hoehner, "Ephesians," 632.

55. Lincoln, *Ephesians*, 42, 235.

56. Utley, "Paul Bound, the Gospel Unbound: Letters from Prison (Colossians, Ephesians and Philemon, Then Later, Philippians)," 44–45.

humanity through Christ (Eph 2:14–17). All three meanings could be present here. However, earlier the writer had said that God, through Christ, had reconciled "to himself all things, whether on earth or in heaven, making peace by the blood of his cross" (1:20). Hence, the peace of Christ to which they were "called" has a soteriological flavor.

But there is an emphasis on the third aspect of peace as well. The writer is probably concerned with peace between the Jewish and Christian factions of the church, as the author of Ephesians was. It is not surprising then that ἐκλήθητε ("you were called") is plural, not singular. Call here is corporate, not individual, and because of that believers need to put on love to uphold the unity that already exists in their call and election. O'Brien[57] goes as far as to assert that "in one body" indicates not the purpose of the believers' calling, but the manner or mode. Either way, call here does not emphasize the freedom of the individual, but the body-life responsibility of each believer as a consequence of their corporate salvation.

4.25 Philippians 3:13–14

Paul, or the one writing in his name, begins chapter 3 by calling the Philippians to rejoice in the Lord, but then warns them about the Judaizing opponents of the gospel (vv. 2–3). In contrast to the Judaizers, Paul has renounced his spiritual and ethnic privileges for the sake of knowing Christ (vv. 4–11); his righteousness comes through Christ, not the law (vv. 12–16). He writes in verse 13:

> Brothers, I do not consider that I have made it my own. But one thing I do: forgetting what lies behind and straining forward to what lies ahead, I press on toward the goal for the prize of the upward call (κλήσεως) of God in Christ Jesus.

The exact meaning of the phrase "the upward call of God" is unclear.[58] It could refer to God's invitation to enter the kingdom (as with 1 Thess 2:12), which is perpetually offered and is ἄνω, "upward," in its action and result. It may refer to an invitation to a life in God's presence—"our heavenward calling." It could refer to the high vocation to which God called all Christians. All these explanations view the genitive τῆς ἄνω κλήσεως τοῦ θεοῦ ("of the upward call of God") as appositional to τὸ βραβεῖον ("the prize"), meaning that the "prize" is identical with God's "call."

---

57. O'Brien, *Colossians, Philemon*, 44, 205.
58. Hawthorne, *Philippians*, 43, 210.

Alternatively, the "upward calling" could refer to the summons given to an athlete to approach the elevated stand of the judge and receive his prize. In which case the phrase could be paraphrased as: "The prize that God, the Judge (ἀγωνοθέτης) will give me when he calls me up and announces my name, the prize that is contained in Christ Jesus"; or "that I may respond to the call, 'come up and receive the prize.'" Debate continues as to which interpretation is correct. If the first one is correct, then we have another example of Paul using call language in a soteriological way.

4.26 Summation

This survey of Paul's use of καλέω shows that it is one of Paul's most important soteriological terms. He uses "call" soteriologically in three ways:

1. In a technical sense (Rom 8:30; Gal 5:8; 1 Thess 5:24).

2. As a substitute for other soteriological terms (Gal 1:6; 1 Cor 1:26–27).

3. In association with a range of other soteriological terms (1 Thess 5:24; 2 Thess 2:14, 1 Cor 1:9).

As a technical term καλέω is the action where "God designates as (or causes to be) a Christian."[59] Paul uses it to mark the point when God applies salvation. Hence, in Paul's usage, the "naming" sense of καλέω is more prominent than the other basic sense of "invite, summon." The causative component present in the "naming" sense of καλέω stresses the act of "appointment to salvation," irrespective of human response, rather than "summons," which implicitly includes the idea of some response.

At the beginning of Paul's earlier Epistles (Galatians, Thessalonians, Corinthians, Romans) he identifies his listeners as "called" before he identifies them as justified, reconciled, redeemed, or adopted. As such, he uses the term as a substitute for other soteriological metaphors.

This prominent use of καλέω could be motivated by the mixed Jewish-Gentile nature of Paul's audiences. He rarely employs terms that could be translated into English using the word "conversion." However, given that calling was analogous to conversion in the ancient Greco-Roman world it serves as a logical substitute in Paul's vocabulary. The fact that "call" language was already "loaded" with soteriological meaning for his Jewish audience as well made it an attractive term for him to use in these early Epistles.

Reflecting its relationship to election and covenant, καλέω marks the status of belonging to God in Pauline Epistles. It denotes the fulfillment in

---

59. Klein, "Paul's Use of Kalein: A Proposal," 63.

the present age of God's pretemporal election, foreknowledge, and predestination. In covenant terms, it specifies the divine act where God creates and names (or designates) people from among Jews and Gentiles to become his own people.[60] Indeed, J. A. Robinson goes as far as equating "calling" with "choosing." He believes that when Paul says, "you were called," he is in effect saying that "God chose you."[61]

But not only does Paul use καλέω in a technical sense for salvation; he uses it alongside a wide range of other soteriological terms. According to Paul, God calls his people to:

- freedom (Gal 5:13)
- love and service (Gal 5:13)
- kingdom and glory (1 Thess 2:12)
- holiness/sanctification (1 Thess 4:7; 5:24, 1 Cor 1:2; Rom 1:7; Eph 4:1; 2 Thess 1:11; 2:14)
- the fellowship of his Son (1 Cor 1:9)
- peace (1 Cor 7:15; Col 3:15)
- one's walk in life (1 Cor 7:17)
- belonging to Jesus Christ (Rom 1:6)
- existence (Rom 4:17)
- justification (Rom 8:30)
- hope (Eph 1:18).

At times Paul uses the fact of God's calling in an imperative sense as an incentive or motivation to act in accordance with the goals God had in mind in calling. At other times, he uses it in an indicative sense simply to exalt the positive benefits of being a recipient of God's calling.[62] Being called also has future results or benefits and present consequences and implications.

God's calling activity reflects his role as creator. For Paul, calling was not just about salvation but the call to a new identity. God calls and God sanctifies. Hence, Paul rarely discusses a human response.

Paul understood his call to apostleship as being a calling to a distinctive task. This is in contrast to the calling of his converts which grants them a new identity understood primarily in terms of who they are, rather than

---

60. *The New Chosen People: A Corporate View of Election*, 228.
61. Robinson, *Commentary on Ephesians*, 90.
62. Klein, "Paul's Use of Kalein: A Proposal," 62.

what they are to do. Their vocation, ethnicity and their past, present or future socioeconomic status is irrelevant.

From this new identity, Paul drew distinct ethical implications. The called are the holy ones who should live a life worthy of the calling. Reflecting his awareness of what the NPP calls covenantal nomism, Paul argues that since God has called people, they have an obligation (calling) to live up to the implications of their status. They are to reflect the ethics of the kingdom, as described in the teachings of Jesus. The Gentile believers are reminded of their freedom that comes from the call, but also the implication that they should no longer conduct themselves in their former ways.

However, the new identity also has communal implications. With the exception of Galatians 1:15 and Romans 9:7, Paul uses calling with a plural object. For Paul, being called also initiates a new identity in terms of belonging to a redeemed community. The self-understanding arising from being called into the fellowship of Christ replaces ethnicity with faith in Christ as the boundary marker.[63] Hence, ethnic differences must not divide the body of Christ nor impose practices on others.

By using calling to denote conversion, Paul has taken an existing soteriological category and modified it for his own purposes to develop a powerful concept to shape the Christian community. The fact that God has called them all to be his people means that their relationship with one another and their relationship with him are inextricably linked. Those called to be saints are separated from their pasts, but called in a new future, separated from those who do not share their calling, but joined to those who do.

In conclusion, Paul's use of καλέω can be summarized in this table:

Concept	References
Related to election	1 Corinthians 1:26; Romans 8:28–30; 9:7, 10–13, 22–26; 2 Thessalonians 2:14
Related to covenant	1 Thessalonians 2:11; 5:24; 1 Corinthians 1:9; Romans 1:6–7, 9:10–13, 22–26, 8:28–30
Related to the kingdom of God	1 Thessalonians 2:12; 2 Thessalonians 1:11
Related to God's eternal purpose of bringing salvation to the Gentiles	Galatians 5:8; 1 Thessalonians 2:11; 1 Corinthians 1:9, Romans 8:28–30; 9:7, 10–13; 11:28–31

---

63. Chester, *Conversion at Corinth*, 111.

Related to sanctification (indicative)	1 Thessalonians 4:7; 5:24; Galatians 5:13; 1 Corinthians 1:2; 2 Thessalonians 1:11
Related to ethics (imperative)	1 Thessalonians 2:11; 4:7, Galatians 5:13; Ephesians 4:1
Present and future experience	2 Thessalonians 2:14
Supersedes ethnicity and socioeconomic status	1 Corinthians 7:15–24
Produces Christian community	1 Corinthians 1:9; Galatians 5:13; 1 Corinthians 1:2; Colossians 3:15
Vocational	1 Corinthians 7:17

5

Luke's Soteriological Use of Call

5.1 Introduction

HAVING REVIEWED PAUL'S SOTERIOLOGICAL use of καλέω, attention now turns to Luke. Luke's soteriological use of this word can be identified in three passages in the Gospel (5:32; 14:12–14, and 14:15–24) and in three passages in Acts (2:21, 39; 15:17). Luke obviously uses καλέω less often than Paul. However, our purpose is not to demonstrate some sort of equivalence in Luke and Paul's usage of the word, simply that they both use it in a similar way in soteriological contexts.

The καλέω words are usually translated as "invite" in the Gospels, reflecting a non-soteriological usage. However, it will be demonstrated that in these passages in Luke and Acts the word is probably being used in a technical and soteriological sense because of the strong allusions to election, covenant, and the messianic banquet.

To begin, it must be acknowledged that Luke does not use καλέω in one notable instance where the other Synoptics do. Mark 3:13 uses προσκαλεῖται ("called to him") to describe the calling of the Twelve and Matthew 10:1 uses προσκαλεσάμενος in the same context. In contrast, Luke (in 6:13) substitutes Mark's προσκαλεῖται with προσεφώνησεν ("called out to his disciples"). However, Luke does use the technical term for election (ἐκλεξάμενος) in his description of the appointing of the apostles in 6:13. There are no clear reasons why Luke deliberately chose to avoid using καλέω here. Nolland describes it as "unmotivated."[1] However, it could be that Luke wished to reserve the term for its technical and soteriological usage later in his Gospel.

---

1. Nolland, *Luke 1:1–9:20*, 35a, 269.

Given that "choice has meaning,"[2] this may be the most plausible explanation for Luke's deliberate choice of words here.

5.2 Luke 5:27–32

Luke 5:27–39 is the fourth and central item in the sevenfold structure of 5:1–6:16.[3] The succession of people on whom Jesus bestows his favor continues. A pattern is repeated (cf. 4:15–30; 5:17–26; 6:1–11; 11:14–54; 13:10–17; 20:1–8) where Jesus and his disciples perform a revolutionary action, the Pharisees remonstrate with him or, on occasion, merely "marvel"—and he makes a pronouncement by which they are silenced.[4] Jesus has shown grace to a demoniac, a leper, and a paralytic; and now we see it given to a tax collector:

> After this he went out and saw a tax collector named Levi, sitting at the tax booth. And he said to him, "Follow me." And leaving everything, he rose and followed him. And Levi made him a great feast (δοχὴν μεγάλην) in his house, and there was a large company of tax collectors and others reclining at table with them. And the Pharisees and their scribes grumbled at his disciples, saying, "Why do you eat and drink with tax collectors and sinners?" And Jesus answered them, "Those who are well have no need of a physician, but those who are sick. I have not come to call (καλέσαι) the righteous but sinners to repentance" (Luke 5:27–32).

This is the first of Luke's several mealtime encounters. There are ten of these feasting scenes in the Gospel, and seven of them are unique to Luke (7:36–50; 10:38–42; 11:37–54; 14:1–24; 19:1–10; 24:29–35, 41–43).

It was common in the Hellenistic world for banquets to be the setting for philosophers and teachers to offer their wisdom. For example, in Plato's *Symposium*, Socrates engages in vigorous discussion in the setting of a banquet.[5] But for Luke, the image of Jesus at a table was that of acceptance for all kinds of people, the proof of which was in sharing a meal.

Jubilees 22:15 reflected the prevailing Jewish ethos when it came to meals: "Keep yourself separate from the nations and do not eat with them . . ." But Jesus was drawing a strange mixture of people around his table

---

2. Lyons, *Introduction to Theoretical Linguistics*, 414.
3. Nolland, *Luke 1:1–9:20*, 35a, 246.
4. Daube, *The New Testament and Rabbinic Judaism*, 170.
5. Hutchins, *Great Books of the Western World*, 149–74.

which caused the religious leaders of Israel to consider him immoral. His inclusiveness, shown most graphically around the meal table, was central to his ministry and its major scandal.[6] The message of Jesus and Luke was that the central symbol of his new vision of life, the kingdom of God, was a community joined together in a festive meal where the bread sustained life and joy.

In Luke's Gospel, Jesus was often a guest at someone's table and many of his most memorable parables were told during a meal. The themes of abundance and hospitality characterized these mealtime parables.[7] Jesus often entered the banquet as one who needed hospitality, but as the banquet proceeded, the role of guest and host were reversed. The meals became places of repentance (5:27–39), reconciliation (7:36–50), and salvation (19:9).

However, Luke's mealtime stories also draw on the imagery of an eschatological banquet in which YHWH "will make for all peoples a feast of rich food," (Isa 25:6). As discussed in Section 2.6, there was an association in the mind of many first-century Jews between great banquets, the covenant, the messiah, and eschatology. The great banquet was viewed as a day of blessing when rich food and wine, symbols of abundant spiritual blessings, would be enjoyed freely (Isa 55:1: "Come, buy wine and milk without money and without price").[8] 2 Baruch 29:3–8 also describes the eschatological banquet:

> And it shall come to pass when all is accomplished that was to come to pass in those parts, that the Messiah shall then begin to be revealed. And Behemoth shall be revealed from his place and Leviathan shall ascend from the sea, those two great monsters which I created on the fifth day of creation, and shall have kept until that time; and then they shall be for food for all that are left. The earth also shall yield its fruit ten-thousandfold and on each vine there shall be a thousand branches, and each branch shall produce a thousand clusters, and each cluster produce a thousand grapes, and each grape produce a cor of wine. And those who have hungered shall rejoice: moreover, also, they shall behold marvels every day. For winds shall go forth from before me to bring every morning the fragrance of aromatic fruits, and at the close of the day clouds distilling the dew of health. And it shall come to pass at that self-same time that the treasury of manna shall again descend from on high, and they will eat of

---

6. Cronshaw, "Mission as Hosting Community Hospitality in Multicultural Australia," 4.

7. Keifert, *Welcoming the Stranger*, 67.

8 Trites and Larkin, *The Gospel of Luke and Acts*, 12, 96.

it in those years, because these are they who have come to the consummation of time.

Luke's emphasis is evident in that, of the evangelists, only he describes this event as a "great banquet" (δοχὴν μεγάλην). Mark only speaks of reclining and eating (Mark 2:15-16), while Matthew (9:9-19) only speaks of Jesus reclining with tax collectors. Luke's choice of this idiom, used in Genesis 21:8 ("And Abraham made a great feast [LXX: δοχὴν μεγάλην] on the day that Isaac was weaned") and Esther 2:18 ("Then the king gave a great feast for all his officials and servants") points to the grandness of the banquet. Jesus, in evocative fashion, placed himself as would-be Messiah in a context where people ate, drank, and celebrated freely (Luke 7:34), bringing to mind the promise of the great eschatological banquet in his audience. The wedding imagery of Luke 5:34 also would have added to the sense of connection between this meal and the great eschatological banquet (see Rev 19:9).

In the context of this "great banquet" Jesus uses "call" terminology: "I have not come to call (καλέσαι) the righteous but sinners to repentance" (5:32). καλέσαι could just be thought of as "invitation." However, as we have seen, καλέσαι is a loaded term, especially in this δοχὴν μεγάλην setting. The atmosphere of the banquet is so charged with salvation imagery that the use of καλέσαι in a soteriological sense is probable.

Jesus could have used different terminology. For example, he could have picked up the language of 19:10 and said, "I have not come to *seek* the righteous." Similarly, he could have simply said, "I have not come to *save* the righteous." This would have been especially tempting given the salvific content of the preceding verse (5:31): "Those who are well have no need of a physician, but those who are sick." Instead he uses καλέσαι, which for his audience would have brought associations with the covenant naming of Israel and the covenant banquets associated with its establishment and consummation.

Nolland suggests that while it would be "tempting" to consider Jesus' call as an invitation to the great eschatological banquet of God, Luke's insertion of "call to repentance" means only a more general sense for "call" may be claimed.[9] However, even though Luke wishes to highlight the concept of repentance, that does not eliminate the clear eschatological banquet and soteriological flavor of this scenario in which the use of καλέσαι would have been evocative. The call to repentance *is* a call to salvation.

It is impossible to be categorical about why Luke chose the words he did. However, it should not be overlooked that he uses call language here in a great banquet setting when he could easily have used σῴζω. Given that

---

9. Nolland, *Luke 1:1–9:20*, 35a, 247.

"choice has meaning," it is most plausible that Jesus and Luke have used "call" here in a technical and soteriological sense. The likelihood of this being the case is reinforced by the usage of the term in Luke 14.

5.3 Luke 14:7–14

This "parable" (14:7) of the wedding feast occurs within the context of Luke's record of the fourth controversy over the Sabbath (cf. 6:1–5; 6:11; 13:10–17). It is obvious that the Sabbath was a major issue between Jesus and the religious leaders. On this Sabbath, Jesus is the guest of a "prominent" (ἀρχόντων) or "ruling" Pharisee, possibly a member of the Sanhedrin. Luke presents the Pharisees and teachers of the law as watchdogs of the faith as they waited for some theological flaw to appear in Jesus' teaching (vv. 1–3; cf. 5:17; 6:7).[10] There appears a man with "dropsy," perhaps "planted" by the Pharisees. As in 6:9, Jesus took the initiative with a question designed to shift the burden of proof to his protagonists (v. 3): "Is it lawful to heal on the Sabbath or not?" During the ensuing silence, Jesus heals the man (v. 4). He says that the guests would help a son or an ox in distress on the Sabbath, so it was totally appropriate to heal this man.

The incident here in 14:1–6 is found only in Luke's Gospel and serves as a literary device to provide a setting for the sayings that follow in Jesus' comments at the dinner table (14:7–24).[11] Jesus' compassion and acceptance of those on the margins is brought into sharp contrast with the exclusivist and judgmental attitude of the Pharisees and teachers of the law. This passage and the following one incorporate several elements—healing, dialogue, and a parable, all tied together in dinner-table conversation, a familiar device in ancient literature.[12] The conversation, except for the account of the healing, revolves around the response and behavior of dinner guests. This leads into the appropriate response of would-be followers of Jesus and the cost of discipleship in 5:35.

There are two parts to this section: one describing the proper etiquette for those invited to a marriage party (14:7–11), and the second part outlining the principles of hospitality for the host who invites the guests (14:12–14).[13]

---

10. Leifeld, "Luke," 976.
11. Trites and Larkin, *The Gospel of Luke and Acts*, 12, 210.
12. Leifeld, "Luke," 976.
13. Trites and Larkin, *The Gospel of Luke and Acts*, 12, 211.

> Now he told a parable to those who were invited (κεκλημένους), when he noticed how they chose the places of honor, saying to them, "When you are invited (κληθῇς) by someone to a wedding feast, do not sit down in a place of honor, lest someone more distinguished than you be invited (κεκλημένος) by him, and he who invited (καλέσας) you both will come and say to you, 'Give your place to this person,' and then you will begin with shame to take the lowest place. But when you are invited (κληθῇς), go and sit in the lowest place, so that when your host comes he may say to you, 'Friend, move up higher.' Then you will be honored in the presence of all who sit at table with you. For everyone who exalts himself will be humbled, and he who humbles himself will be exalted" (Luke 14:7–11).

As well as being placed in the same mealtime context, the καλέω cognates (14:7, 8, 9, 10, 12, 13, 16, 17, and 24) link the elements of Luke 14:7–24 into a unit. "καλέω is the key word which holds the whole of this section together."[14] Certainly the parables require the non-technical use of the term. However, the prevalence of καλέω language throughout these units means that it is also being used as a connecting thematic motif. This suggests that it is being used in a technical and soteriological sense. This argument is reinforced by the theme related to call that underlies the chapter—election, as will now be explained.

The teaching moment came out of the selfish jockeying for "seats of honor near the head of the table" (14:7). The parable is based on the practice of seating guests at the table by rank and distinction. The more important guests would arrive last, and an early arrival might result in being moved to a lower place so as to accommodate them. It is better to adopt a position of modesty and wait to be invited to a better seat "for God exalts the humble and humbles the proud."[15] The saying is clearly aimed at the Pharisees and teachers of the law who, with their sense of superiority, have placed themselves in the highest seats at the banquet.

The second piece of etiquette advice relates to the choice of guests:

> He said also to the man who had invited him, "When you give a dinner (ἄριστον) or a banquet (δεῖπνον), do not invite (φώνει) your friends or your brothers or your relatives or rich neighbors, lest they also invite you in return (ἀντικαλέσωσίν) and you be repaid. But when you give a feast (δοχήν), invite (κάλει) the poor, the crippled, the lame, the blind, and you will be blessed,

---

14. Marshall, *Commentary on Luke*, 581.
15. Carson et al., *New Bible Commentary: 21st Century Edition*, 1004.

because they cannot repay you. For you will be repaid at the resurrection of the just" (Luke 14:12–14).

The host is advised not to give a banquet for his friends, relatives, colleagues, and neighbors. These people would undoubtedly reciprocate, and, following the laws of conventional courtesy, in the course of time, repay the hospitality in a similar way.[16] This saying challenges the exclusivism of the religious leaders in contrast to Jesus' practice of accepting and embracing the marginalized.

Although the parable may be interpreted as just a lesson in kingdom social ethics, there is an underlying theme of election. Luke's purpose was to show his readers why the Pharisees' and teachers' lack of repentance led both to their exclusion from the people of God and to the events of 70 CE.[17] The Pharisees and teachers of the law were overconfident in their status of election based on their ethnic and social identity. But the nation of Israel had not been elected because of their greatness, but simply in the sovereignty of YHWH. Instead of seeing it as election for the purpose of mission and compassion, the Pharisees and teachers of the law had come to see it as a basis of ethnic and social superiority.

This sense of superiority not only colored the Pharisees' and teacher's attitude to the Gentiles, but also to their fellow Israelites. The Gentiles were, of course, excluded from inner courts of the temple. However, the outcasts of Israel, including the poor and crippled and blind and lame, were also excluded from the temple (Lev 21:17–23; 2 Sam 5:8) and the atoning sacrificial system associated with it. The elitism of the Pharisees and teachers was not only sociological, but also religious. Hence, Jesus' inclusion of such people in the banquet and the lessons he draws from the banquet have a distinctly soteriological flavor.

In the Nazareth Manifesto (Luke 4:17–19; Isa 61), Luke reports that Jesus' mission is to proclaim the gospel to the poor, captive, blind, and oppressed. The hypothetical host's invitation/call of the poor, crippled, lame, and blind in 14:13 resonates with Jesus' salvific mission statement. The call of these "nobodies" echoes God's election of Israel who were at one time just a mob of slaves in Egypt. Israel is described in Isaiah 41:9 (LXX) as: "You whom I took from the ends of the earth, and called (ἐκάλεσα) from its farthest corners." Yet the Pharisees and teachers of the law had forgotten this aspect of divine election. The result was the sharp clash of ideologies between the religious leaders and Jesus.

---

16. Trites and Larkin, *The Gospel of Luke and Acts*, 12, 212.
17. Stein, *Luke*, 391.

This underlying theme of the misunderstanding of election is further developed in Luke's next episode.

5.4 Luke 14:15-24

The mention of the resurrection in verse 14 and the eschatological flavor of the whole scene prompted one of the guests to comment on the happy situation of the people who would share in the heavenly banquet (v. 15): "When one of those who reclined at table with him heard these things, he said to him, 'Blessed is everyone who will eat bread in the kingdom of God!'"

In response Jesus speaks another parable:

> But he said to him, "A man once gave a great banquet (δεῖπνον μέγα) and invited (ἐκάλεσεν) many. And at the time for the banquet he sent his servant to say to those who had been invited (κεκλημένοις), 'Come, for everything is now ready.' But they all alike began to make excuses. The first said to him, 'I have bought a field, and I must go out and see it. Please have me excused.' And another said, 'I have bought five yoke of oxen, and I go to examine them. Please have me excused.' And another said, 'I have married a wife, and therefore I cannot come.' So the servant came and reported these things to his master. Then the master of the house became angry and said to his servant, 'Go out quickly to the streets and lanes of the city, and bring in the poor and crippled and blind and lame.' And the servant said, 'Sir, what you commanded has been done, and still there is room.' And the master said to the servant, 'Go out to the highways and hedges and compel (ἀνάγκασον) people to come in, that my house may be filled. For I tell you, none of those men who were invited (κεκλημένων) shall taste my banquet (δείπνου)'" (Luke 14:16-24).

The use of ἐκάλεσεν connects the parable to the surrounding elements and suggests a soteriological theme. One must not make too much of Luke's alternate use of "compel" (ἀνάγκασον) in 14:23. The use of force to bring people to salvation is not advocated. The reason for the use of ἀνάγκασον is that in the Middle East the unexpected invitation must be refused.[18] The refusal is all the more required if the guest is of lower social rank than the host, as with the case of the outcasts in the story. On the Emmaus Road (Luke 24:13-35) Jesus receives an unexpected invitation. As a courteous

---

18. Bailey, *Through Peasant Eyes: A Literary-Cultural Approach to the Parables in Luke*, 108.

Middle Easterner he "acted as if he were going further" (24:28). The two men, again in true Middle Eastern fashion, "urged him strongly" (24:29) to stay. He is not forced against his will. Rather, they know he must initially refuse as a matter of honor. Similarly, in this parable, a stranger from outside the city is suddenly invited to a great banquet. The servant will have to be quite persistent to convince the guest to come to a banquet so clearly above their social class, hence the use of ἀνάγκασον.

A very similar parable to Luke 14:15–24 appears in Matthew 22:1–14 and in the Gospel of Thomas 64. It is generally accepted that the three parables are variants of one original parable, which is close to the Lukan version.[19] However, the differences between the two parables in Luke and Matthew are striking: in Luke the story concerns "a certain man," while in Matthew it concerns "a king." Luke describes a δεῖπνον (meal) in contrast to Matthew who describes it as a γάμος (wedding banquet) given by a king for his son. In Luke there is one invitation, in Matthew two. In Luke the invited guests make excuses, in Matthew the excuses are summarized and the invited guests turn violent. In Luke the invited guests are passed by, in Matthew they are destroyed. Luke has a servant or herald deliver the calls while Matthew has an army. Luke's new guests are specifically named as the poor, maimed, blind, and lame (as in 14:13). Matthew describes the newly-called guests as "all you can find" or simply as "both bad and good."

The diversity is such that one might validly conclude that Matthew and Luke record two different parables, given in their respective settings, stemming from two historical situations. It is certainly plausible that Jesus preached similar parables in different settings. For example, the observation that Matthew's parable is harsher than Luke's may owe much to the historical situation. In Matthew, it is open confrontation with the Jewish leaders during Passion Week, while Luke's mealtime setting is earlier and less adversarial. Certainly, each parable makes admirable sense in its own setting.[20]

As to whether Matthew and Luke received this parable in the same form, or whether it was two different traditions, Nolland concludes that in the end we cannot be sure.[21] Either way, comparing the two parables in Matthew and Luke does shed some light on the reasons they chose the tradition they did, or how they have redacted the same tradition in the way they have.

---

19. Marshall, *Commentary on Luke*, 584.
20. Carson, "Matthew," 455–6.
21. Nolland, *Luke 1:1–9:20*, 35a, 754.

Two key messages can be discerned from the parable in Luke 14: the concept of Israel's misunderstanding of election and that the messianic meal had begun.

5.4.1 Israel's Misunderstanding of Election

Difficulties in attempting to interpret the parables emerge from attempting to take the story in too literal a sense in order to construct a coherent allegory, whether at the level of Jesus' original intention or the evangelist's interpretation.[22] Hence, Marshall argues that it is best to simply see this parable as a story where Jesus comments on "pious" Israel who neither entered the kingdom themselves nor allowed others to enter. They are warned they will be excluded from the kingdom and that it will be offered instead to the needy and outsiders. Subsequently, Marshall asserts that the elements of substitution and succession should not be pressed in the interpretation and that an allusion to Gentile mission is possible, but not the main focus of the message. The invitation may be taken to represent God's call to Israel, given in various ways, and not necessarily restricted to one particular group of people.

However, the threefold mission paradigm which unfolds across Luke–Acts is readily observable in the parable: following Israel's rejection the gospel goes to the outcasts of Israel (the streets and lanes *of the city* to bring in the poor and crippled and blind and lame), and then to the Gentiles (the highways and hedges *outside* the city). Although there is no reference to ethnicity in the story, the three-stage mission interpretation of the parable would fit with the overall structure of Luke–Acts.

This threefold expansion is also expressed in the later parable of the Vineyard (20:9–16) and echoes the "Jerusalem, Judea and ends of the earth" expression in Acts 1:8. Further, it is reasonable to link the parable with the preceding saying in Luke 13:28–30 ("And people will come from east and west, and from north and south, and recline at table in the kingdom of God") and find in it an allusion to the extension of the gospel to the Gentiles. The last two points of the compass are Luke's addition to east and west (Matt 8:11) to emphasize the universality of the kingdom.

Finally, the servant in the parable does not actually go out to the outsiders (Gentiles) along the highways and by the hedges.[23] The command is given, but not carried out. This parallels Jesus' own ministry in that he

---

22. Marshall, *Commentary on Luke*, 587.

23. Bailey, *Through Peasant Eyes: A Literary-Cultural Approach to the Parables in Luke*, 101.

did carry out a ministry of inviting the outcasts of Israel into his fellowship. The commission regarding the Gentiles was only fulfilled in Acts after his ascension. Luke demonstrated God's intent to call the Gentiles (see Luke 2:32) and if the threefold invitation of the parable is interpreted in this light it makes perfect sense.[24]

So, it is reasonable to assume that Luke's message in this chapter is that rejection of Jesus and the kingdom by "the elect" (14:24) leads to the call of Israel's outcasts (4:18; 7:22) and the Gentiles (Acts 13:47-48; 18:6; 28:25-28). Israel has rejected her election (call) and now God has elected the outcasts and the Gentiles.

> The rejection of the gospel by Israel's leadership would not thwart God's plan. Those like the Pharisee in the account who believed they were guaranteed a place in the kingdom had excluded themselves (14:18-20) and would not participate (Luke 14:24), but God's plan would be fulfilled nevertheless. The first were indeed last (13:30); those who exalted themselves had been humbled (14:11).[25]

In the OT Israel is often reminded that she was once a slave people and so must always be conscious of the poor and powerless in order to continue to be God's covenant people (14:29; 16:11-14). Luke's parable reflects a call from Jesus to remember this basic concept.

Indeed, Luke understood that Jesus' purpose in this parable was a prophetic critique of the contemporary understanding of the Deuteronomic understanding of election.[26] He stood in the tradition of the eighth-century prophets in pointing Israel back towards covenant faithfulness. Deuteronomy 18:15, the promise of the prophet like Moses, is at the heart of what Luke wants to say about Jesus in this section: "The LORD your God will raise up for you a prophet like me from among you, from your brothers—it is to him you shall listen."

In attempting to explain the structure and content of the central section of Luke's Gospel (9:51-18:43) a number of different models have been suggested. One model is that Luke follows the general order of Deuteronomy by using catchwords easily traced in the LXX.[27] Evans is able to match each section of Deuteronomy to the central section (9:51-18:43) of Luke. Some of the more obvious parallels include:

---

24. Crabbe, "Transforming Tables: Meals as Encounters with the Kingdom in Luke," 100.
25. Stein, *Luke*, 394-5.
26. Sanders, "The Ethic of Election in Luke's Great Banquet Parable," 265.
27. Evans, *Saint Luke*, 34-36.

Deut 1: Israel journeys from Horeb to Canaan under Moses, who sends twelve men in advance	Luke 10: 1–3, 17–30: Jesus journeys from the Mount to Jerusalem, and appoints seventy to be sent in advance
Deut 2—3:22: Moses sends messengers of peace to Sihon and Og, who on rejecting are destroyed	Luke 10:4–16: The seventy sent with a message of peace; destruction on those who reject
Deut 5—6: The Decalogue summarized in the *shema*. Observance brings inheritance and land and life	Luke 10:25–27: The *shema* with love of the neighbor brings inheritance of eternal life
Deut 7: Have no mercy on the foreigner lest he corrupt from true worship	Luke 10:29–37: Parable of the Good Samaritan
Deut 12:1–16: Clean and unclean	Luke 11:37–12:2: Clean and unclean
Deut 14:28: Tithe every third year	Luke 13:6–9: A vineyard unfruitful for three years
Deut 15:1–18: Release from debt and slavery every seventh year	Luke 13:10–21: Release on the Sabbath of a woman from bondage to Satan
Deut 20: Exemption from battle for those who have built a house, planted a vineyard or married. Offer peace before destroying an enemy	Luke 14:15–35: Parable of the Great Feast; those who give excuses excluded. Counting the cost in building a tower or waging war
Deut 21:15–22:4: Father and son. In the division of inheritance, the firstborn to be given his right. The rebellious son to be stoned. Restoration of anything the brother has lost	Luke 15:1–32: Parables of Lost Sheep and Lost Coin teaching joy over repentant sinners. Parable of two sons, firstborn and rebellious, the latter received back with joy
Deut 24:6–25:3: Injunctions against oppressive treatment of the poor. Take heed of leprosy. In harvest leave a sheaf for the alien. Judges to justify the righteous	Luke 16:19–18:8: Vindication of the poor in the judgement. Parable of rich man and Lazarus. Healing of lepers. The kingdom of God is among you. Parable of unjust judge

Despite some criticisms, studies have tended to confirm the validity of viewing the Lucan portrait of Jesus against the background of Deuteronomy and Moses.[28] Whether or not Deuteronomy is the basis of the structure and content of the central section of Luke, "there are undoubted reminiscences of Deuteronomy throughout Luke."[29] It is plausible to think of the relationship between the central section of Luke and Deuteronomy as something more than a stylistic device intended to provide further proof that Jesus was the Deuteronomistic prophet. The Deuteronomic backdrop could help Luke to clarify a significant theological point that he was trying to make.

28. Evans, "Luke's Use of the Elijah/Elisha Narratives and the Ethic of Election," 76.
29. Marshall, *Commentary on Luke*, 589.

In particular, this Deuteronomistic backdrop provides a basis for the interpretation of the parable of the Great Banquet. The specific link is that the three excuses the invited guests make are based on the four causes for deferment from serving in war recorded in Deuteronomy 20:5–8. However, the obvious connections between Deuteronomy and the central section of Luke mean that it is a useful tool for interpretation even if the three excuses do not provide a specific link.

The Deuteronomistic backdrop lends weight to the idea that Luke is concerned with the Pharisees' and scribes' misunderstanding of election and the implications it has for their behavior towards the outcast and the Gentiles. Luke is pointing out that God reserves the right to designate those who are the elect by calling whoever he likes to the great banquet. God also reserves the right to reject those who consider themselves the elect. As the host, God has the right to alter the guest list at will. God can indeed be angry at the "elect" (Luke 14:21) and execute power and freedom in favor of whom he wishes.[30]

Sanders concludes:

> The theme of the Central Section of Luke's Gospel is that the Deuteronomic ethic of election has been subverted: Whereas Deuteronomy stressed that obedience brings blessings and disobedience curses, one cannot go on to assume (as many ever since Deuteronomy did assume—see the book of Job) that suffering indicates one is not elect while riches or ease on earth indicates that one is elect.[31]

This error is what Jesus seeks to address in the parables of the Great Banquet, the Prodigal Son and the Rich Man, and Lazarus. These parables are a teaching on humility and a prophetic critique of a common *inversion* of the Deuteronomic ethic of election.

> Deuteronomy may well say that God blesses the obedient and judges the disobedient. But it does *not* say that poverty and affliction and lack of bodily wholeness are proof of God's disfavor. On the contrary, these Lukan constructions appear to insist on a common Old Testament theme that God has a kind of bias for those in apparent disfavor.[32]

Hence, τῶν κεκλημένων in Luke are not "the elect" but the "*apparently* elect/called" or "those who consider themselves elect/called." Like

---

30. Sanders, "The Ethic of Election in Luke's Great Banquet Parable," 261.
31. Ibid., 258.
32. Ibid., 265.

the classical prophets of the OT, Jesus challenges assumptions concerning election, concluding: "I tell you, none of the men who were invited (τῶν κεκλημένων) shall taste my banquet" (14:24).

This interpretation is supported by comparison with Matthew and the Gospel of Thomas. Only in Luke are the new invitations extended specifically to the poor, crippled, blind, and lame (14:21), an allusion to Israel's inauspicious origins and a reminder of the need for humility in election.

However, this is not the only message in the parable of Luke 14:16–24.

5.4.2 The Messianic Banquet Has Begun

Alongside the theme of election in the parable is its eschatological flavor. Although Luke may have had several purposes for his Gospel, as has already been demonstrated in the earlier sections of this chapter, he is keen to emphasize the messianic banquet dimensions of Jesus' mealtime encounters and words.

Although the meal in this parable is not specifically identified as a messianic banquet, the comment of the diner in verse 15 indicates that the sayings and meal setting have clearly brought it to mind. And although Jesus corrects the diner, he focuses on correcting incorrect assumptions about the character of the kingdom, not rejecting the observation that the setting has eschatological implications. While sounding devout, the statement assumes that God's kingdom is a distant abstraction rather than, as Jesus had been teaching, a present reality brought about by his coming.[33]

A number of elements accentuate the eschatological themes of the meal.[34] The divine passives of the preceding sayings stress the ultimate action of God. The meal setting itself, in light of earlier type-scenes and the background material discussed above, is primed with eschatological imagery. The mention of elevation of the poor, blind, crippled, and lame echoes Luke 4:18–19 and Isaiah 61 and further contributes to the eschatological feel.

Although Jesus refers to the meal as a δεῖπνον, the word used for the main meal of the day, it could also refer to a cultic meal as it is here.[35] For example, in the NT it is used at the Passover referred to in John 13:4, 21:20, and 1 Corinthians 11:20.

---

33. Stein, *Luke*, 392.

34. Crabbe, "Transforming Tables: Meals as Encounters with the Kingdom in Luke," 98.

35. Arndt et al., *A Greek-English Lexicon of the New Testament and Other Early Christian Literature*, 215.

As Stein writes:

> The parable fits well the Lukan emphasis on the realized nature of God's kingdom. When the Pharisee spoke of the kingdom as a future abstraction (Luke 14:15), he stood in direct contradiction to Jesus' preaching that God's kingdom had come. Jesus' central message (and John the Baptist's before him) was the arrival of that awaited kingdom.[36]

Bailey concludes: "Here as elsewhere the banquet is a symbol for salvation."[37] The messianic banquet promised by Isaiah (Isa 25:6–9) is inaugurated in the table fellowship of Jesus. Indeed, the "hour of the banquet" (14:17) has come. But those who seek to "eat bread in the kingdom of God" initially must seek to eat bread with Jesus.[38] Those invited/called (the leaders of the Jewish community) are told, "All is now ready." Yet there are a series of excuses from the characters in the parable and the Pharisees and teachers of the law who listen to it. The Pharisees and teachers reject the invitation to the banquet of salvation set for them through the presence of Jesus in their midst because Jesus eats with and welcomes sinners and does not keep the Sabbath. As noted above, the Qumran community anticipated a rejection from the messianic banquet of everyone who was "smitten in his flesh . . . or lame, or blind." The Pharisees seemed to have held similar beliefs. Deeper reasons for his rejection may be that he did not fulfil their theological and nationalistic expectations of the Messiah. Either way, their rejection of the call to attend the banquet with Jesus had eschatological and soteriological consequences.

The nature of this messianic banquet is worth noting. Braun[39] draws on social and literary evidence regarding the Greco-Roman elite banquet scene and on ancient prescribed methods of rhetorical composition to argue that the episode in Luke 14 is a crafted rhetorical unit in which Jesus presents an argument for Luke's vision of a Christian society. The picture of the banquet in Luke 14 is paradigmatic of the kingdom. It is an egalitarian gathering of a very "mixed" collection of people enjoying the hospitality of the Messiah. The socioeconomic status of the participants is no longer relevant.

---

36. Stein, *Luke*, 394–5.

37. Bailey, *Through Peasant Eyes: A Literary-Cultural Approach to the Parables in Luke*, 89.

38. Ibid., 99.

39. Braun, *Feasting and Social Rhetoric in Luke 14*.

5.4.3 Summation

Certainly, this parable is directed at the Pharisees and teachers to remind them of the humility that they should exercise as a result of the election of Israel, rather than the proud condemnation of sinners they demonstrate. As such, it is a parable about the misunderstanding of election. However, its strong eschatological flavor cannot be ignored. Alongside the theme of election, and intertwined with it, is the message that the kingdom of God has been initiated and that the Messiah is actively "calling" the devout, the outcast, and the Gentile to enter the eschatological banquet. Hence, it is also a parable about God's offer of salvation.

Luke proclaims the present reality of the kingdom of God in Jesus' ministry and that to reject Jesus' announcement of the arrival of the kingdom is to miss sharing in both its present realization (the banquet where the parable is spoken) and its future consummation (the messianic banquet).

Having examined Luke's use of καλέω in his Gospel we now move to an examination of its soteriological use in Acts.

5.5 Acts 2:39

According to Luke, at the conclusion of his Pentecost sermon, Peter says:

> And it shall come to pass that everyone who calls (ἐπικαλέσηται)
> upon the name of the Lord shall be saved (Acts 2:21).

In Luke's allusion to Joel 2:32, he is clearly linking call to salvation. Although, in this case, the call comes from the human rather than God, the usage is still clearly soteriological. After the crowd interjects with the question, Peter continues in Acts 2:38–39:

> And Peter said to them, "Repent and be baptized every one of you in the name of Jesus Christ for the forgiveness of your sins, and you will receive the gift of the Holy Spirit. For the promise is for you and for your children and for all who are far off, everyone whom the Lord our God calls (προσκαλέσηται) to himself."

The opportunity to call on the name of the Lord and be saved extends not only to the Jews but to those who are far off—the Gentiles. The "promise" of which Peter speaks includes both the forgiveness of sins and the gift of the Holy Spirit.[40] It is not only for his immediate hearers ("for you") but also for succeeding generations ("for your children") and for all in distant

---

40. Longenecker, "The Acts of the Apostles," 285.

places ("for all who are far off"). The call of God is not just for ancient Israel but for every generation and people.

In this passage, Luke puts together the human side of salvation ("repent and be baptized") and the divine side ("God calls to himself"). At the very least, call is here being used soteriologically and it is quite plausible that it is being used as a substitute for σῴζει ("saves") in this context.

5.6 Acts 15:17

At the Council of Jerusalem James says:

> "Brothers, listen to me. Simeon has related how God first visited the Gentiles, to take from them a people for his name. And with this the words of the prophets agree, just as it is written,
> 'After this I will return,
>   and I will rebuild the tent of David that has fallen;
> I will rebuild its ruins,
>   and I will restore it,
> that the remnant of mankind may seek the Lord,
>   and all the Gentiles who are called (ἐπικέκληται) by my name,
> says the Lord, who makes these things known from of old'"
> (Acts 15:13–18).

Luke has James quoting Amos 9:11–12 which looked to the time when God would restore the house of David. He uses the LXX translation of the text, which in contrast to the Masoretic text reads "they may seek" for "they will inherit" and "of mankind" for "of Edom." James could well have quoted the LXX because it fitted his purpose of expressing the universal nature of God's promise of salvation. However, the Hebrew text of Amos 9:12 may be translated, "That they may possess the remnant of Edom and all the nations who are called by my name."[41] If so, it also carries the more universalistic flavor.

Either way, James concurred with Peter that the time of Gentile inclusion in God's people had arrived. The restoration of David's kingdom clearly has covenantal and soteriological connotations. The "calling" of the Gentiles does not contradict the Old Testament prophets. Those called by God's name are in a saving relationship with him.[42] Again, we can see Luke's use of call in a soteriological sense.

---

41. Toussaint, "Acts," 394.
42. Dennis and Grudem, *The ESV Study Bible*, 2115.

5.7 Summation

Luke uses καλέω language in his Gospel and in Acts with a distinctly soteriological flavor. In Acts, he records Peter and James using call terminology as they quote OT passages referring to salvation. In Luke 5, he uses καλέω in parallel with salvation and chooses it instead of a range of other words. In Luke 14, καλέω language is prevalent and unifies the three sections in which it is used and suggests it technical use. The sequence of events is charged with eschatological and soteriological imagery. He particularly portrays the meal in Luke 14 as the eschatological messianic covenant banquet. Luke's message through this imagery is that the kingdom of God has arrived. To reject Jesus' announcement of the arrival of the kingdom is to miss sharing in both its present realization (the banquet where the parable is spoken) and its future consummation (the messianic banquet).

Further, God continues to call the unlikely to salvation in his sovereign program of election. Although he had elected and called Israel they had misunderstood its implications. Further, they were now rejecting the Messiah and so God was electing to call the outcasts of Israel and the Gentiles.

The threefold extension of the gospel from the Jews, to the Samaritans, and to the end of the earth, is a key theme of Luke–Acts. The author portrays this as a response to Jewish unbelief and the Messiah, but it is still part of God's salvation purposes. The newly redefined messianic banquet is composed not of the Jewish elect but the outcasts of Jewish society and the Gentiles. As such, the ethnic and social boundaries which once discriminated and excluded, have been dissolved by Jesus.

The product of the dissolution of these boundaries is a community of the called. Certainly, an individual must repent to be saved, but there are no passages in the Synoptics that refer to God's choice of a specific individual salvation.[43] Apart from the few references to God's choice of Jesus and the apostles, individual election does not occur. In these cases, the choosing was for mission, not salvation. Similarly, in Acts, Luke never uses the verb ἐκλέγομαι (choose, elect) to refer to God's choice of individual people for salvation. People are called to a messianic banquet and banquets by their very nature are communal. And so, salvation for Luke is a call to a community united around the table of Jesus, with the story of Zacchaeus and the imagery of the banquet in Luke 14 as the type examples.

Although Luke does not use the language of sanctification, he does use a related concept. For Luke, salvation and its related concept, call, are connected to repentance and the reception of the Holy Spirit. However,

---

43. Klein, *The New Chosen People: A Corporate View of Election*, 103–13.

Luke's concept of repentance means more than turning away from sin, but embarking upon a new life in accordance with the kingdom as illustrated by the story of Zacchaeus.

The following table summarizes Luke's soteriology, for comparison with the summary of Paul above:

Concept	Reference
Related to salvation	Luke 5:31–32
Related to election	Luke 14:7–11, 16–24
Related to covenant (through the image of the eschatological banquet)	Luke 14:12–14; Acts 2:21, 39; 15:17
Related to the kingdom of God	Luke 14:15; Acts 15:17
Related to God's eternal purpose to take salvation to the Gentiles	Luke 14:16–24; Acts 2:21, 39; 15:17
Related to repentance	Luke 5:27–32
Present and future experience	Luke 14:24
Supersedes ethnicity and socioeconomic status	Luke 14:16–24
Produces Christian community	Luke 14:16–24

6

Conclusions

6.1 Introduction

THIS BOOK HAS SOUGHT to tackle the question: "What role does the call (καλέω) of God play in the soteriologies of Paul and Luke?" And so, I have attempted to examine the soteriological use of καλέω and its cognates in Luke–Acts and the Pauline corpus and to draw conclusions and implications from its use. The following conclusions can be drawn from this examination and will be discussed further in this chapter:

1. καλέω language is an important concept in the soteriologies of Luke and Paul.

2. Although there are contrasts, there are a number of points of comparison in the soteriological use of καλέω by Luke and Paul. Crucial to this common understanding is the association of καλέω language with the Old Testament covenants, election, covenant meals, and an expectation of the eschatological banquet.

3. As a result of this prominent and consistent usage by Paul and Luke, the language of καλέω deserves a higher place in the Christian understanding of salvation. This has implications for Christian life and practice.

6.2 Call in New Testament Soteriology

I have sought to demonstrate that, despite its omission or downplaying in many systematic discussions of soteriology in the NT, καλέω is a significant soteriological concept in the theologies of Luke and Paul. Although scholars have long recognized the usage of καλέω as a term for the summons or invitation to salvation, it deserves an elevated position in the pantheon of soteriological concepts.[1]

Paul uses the language of call frequently in his Epistles and often places it in crucial locations in his argument. He uses the term early in Galatians, 1 Thessalonians, 1 Corinthians, and Romans, and always before that of other soteriological categories such as justification, adoption, and redemption.

Luke also reports Jesus using καλέω language in soteriological sense. Although the usage is less frequent in Luke–Acts, its use is strategic. Jesus uses call language synonymously with salvation and in the banquet setting of Luke 14 he uses the term in a clearly soteriological sense. Given the "vagueness" of Luke with respect to the "how" of salvation, the importance of his use of this covenantal term in these settings should not be underestimated.

One suggestion to explain the prominent place that καλέω has for both Paul and Luke is the accessibility of the concept for Gentiles. Unlike other OT soteriological categories such as righteousness and covenant, "call" language had a preexisting association with conversion in the ancient Greco-Roman world. This made it particularly attractive for Paul in communicating with his Gentile audience and perhaps also explains why Jesus uses it as he talks about the unfolding salvation plan of God reaching the Gentiles in Luke 14 and other places in the Synoptic Gospels.

However, we have also demonstrated the long history of καλέω language with the salvation tradition of the Jewish faith. It reaches right back to the call of Abraham through the "call" language employed in the covenants, through to the prophetic declarations of the postexilic era. One of the central themes in the OT is the covenant relationship between YHWH and "his people." Associated with this is the LXX's use of καλέω and its cognates in association with the election of Abraham and the nation of Israel. As such, the concept of call was a familiar and warm one for Paul and Jesus and one which they naturally used in their communication. Although Luke was a Gentile, there is ample evidence in Luke–Acts of his extensive awareness of the OT, and, possibly, the tutorage of Jewish Christ-followers such as Paul.

The New Perspective on Paul has moved covenant more towards the center of Paul's soteriology. A greater appreciation of the importance of καλέω language is consistent with this development. Salvation for Paul is a much broader concept than the imputation of righteousness and greater attention should be paid to metaphors such as adoption, covenant, and calling.

1. See Hussey, "The Soteriological Use of 'Call' in the New Testament: An Undervalued Category?"

καλέω language brings its own unique contribution to the rich tapestry of soteriology in the NT. In particular, calling emphasizes the initiative of God in salvation. No fallen human ever called themselves.[2] God always takes the initiative. He always brings the covenant to the elect. He calls/names his people in the covenant process and they are his. This realization brings with it the appropriate response of living a life worthy of the call. Call language also brings with it the expectation of a call to something. It is in thus a more "active" category of salvation than imputed righteousness.

Some readers may be disappointed that this book has not dealt in depth with a "hot topic" of systematic theology: predestination. This has been to some extent by deliberate choice but also by the fact that it does not emerge immediately out of the biblical theological approach undertaken in this research. As Marshall writes:

> We have not found any clear evidence in these epistles to support the view that the elect are a body of specific individuals chosen before the foundation of the world to be effectually called and to attain to final salvation without any possibility of their falling away. Paul certainly believed that his confidence had every ground for confidence in God; he did not replace this relationship of personal trust with the inevitability of an impersonal deterministic system. To do so is to press Paul's statements into a logical framework which he himself does not appear to have held, and to create fresh problems of understanding.[3]

The language of καλέω is certainly associated with the predestination/free will debate. However, Luke and Paul did not use καλέω for the purpose of clarifying the process of salvation. Their intention was more significant than this. It was to add a rich metaphor to their reader's understanding of salvation which was not only familiar to Jew and Gentile but which also motivated them towards ethical and communal life.

6.3 Call and the Soteriologies of Luke and Paul

Soteriology has been identified by many scholars as one of the "wedges" which separate the theologies of Paul and Luke. We have seen that when Paul and Luke use the term καλέω in their writings they sometimes do so in the technical sense relating to salvation. Rather than being something that divides their theologies, their technical usage of καλέω language is

---

2. Utley, "Romans 1:7."
3. Marshall, "Election and Calling to Salvation in 1 and 2 Thessalonians," 276.

something that actually unites them. Indeed, there are a number of points where they not only use καλέω language, but do so in similar theological contexts and with similar purposes.

The commonality in Paul and Luke's use of καλέω language is summarized in this table:

Concept	Luke	Paul
Related to election	Luke 14:7–11, 16–24	1 Corinthians 1:26; Romans 8:28–30; 9:7, 10–13, 22–26; 2 Thessalonians 2:14
Related to covenant	Luke 14:12–14	1 Thessalonians 5:24; 1 Corinthians 1:9; Romans 1:6–7; 9:10–13, 22–26; 8:28–30
Related to the kingdom of God	Luke 14:15; Acts 15:17	1 Thessalonians 2:12; 2 Thessalonians 1:5, 11
Related to God's eternal purpose to take salvation to the Gentiles	Luke 14:16–24; Acts 2:21, 39; 15:17	Galatians 5:8; 1 Thessalonians 2:11; 1 Corinthians 1:9; Romans 8:28–30; 9:7, 10–13; 11:28–31
Related to sanctification/repentance	Luke 5:27–32	1 Thessalonians 2:11; 4:7; Galatians 5:13; Ephesians 4:1
Present and future experience	Luke 14:15–24	2 Thessalonians 2:14
Supersedes ethnicity and socioeconomic status	Luke 14:16–24	1 Corinthians 7:15–24
Produces Christian community	Luke 14:16–24	Galatians 5:13; 1 Corinthians 1:2, 9

Admittedly, two aspects of Paul's use of καλέω (the indicative sense of sanctification and vocation) are not readily observable in Luke–Acts. This should not be surprising given the different authors' intention in their different contexts. Luke's use of καλέω in this soteriological manner is more subtle than that of Paul. However, Paul's more extensive use of the language should not be used to suggest a difference between the two writers. Because Luke is using narrative to teach his theology, statistical frequency of his use of the term should not be used as a distinguishing mark.

The first commonality in the usage of καλέω by Luke and Paul is its connection with election. Although Luke does not use the same soteriological terminology and metaphors as those Paul uses in his Epistles, there is at least one common thread—the concept of election and participation in a covenant relationship with God. This common understanding is reflected by the use of the term καλέω.

Although using proposition instead of story, Paul reaches the same conclusion about election and Israel as Luke. The misunderstanding of the doctrine of Deuteronomic election highlighted by Luke 14 is exactly what Paul is addressing in Romans 9. In Romans, Paul describes how Israel has rejected their Messiah and so placed their election in jeopardy. Similarly, Luke 14 shows how the guests have placed their invitation in jeopardy by their rejection of the Messiah. For Paul, there is still hope for Israel, but this time through the election of the Gentiles. Jesus and Luke would seem to express no such optimism. However, if the parable is seen to be a warning to the Jews, not the judgment, it could still express hope of their acceptance of the Messiah.

In light of this, it is not unreasonable to assert that call was a soteriological metaphor which was in the mind of both Jesus and Paul when they sought to describe the election of the Gentiles. The idea of "Those who were once not my people are now my people" may have been the OT stimulus for both.

Both Paul and Luke use καλέω language when they talk about, or allude to, the covenants. As evidenced by the similar accounts of the Lord's Supper in Luke and 1 Corinthians, Paul and Luke shared a common understanding of the covenantal implications of Jesus' last meal with the disciples. Whether Luke had in mind a vicarious sacrifice or not, Jesus' death was clearly covenantal in nature. This common understanding of the importance of the relationship between covenant and salvation explains the technical usage of καλέω in other parts of their writings.

Paul and Luke also use καλέω language when they are seeking to explain God's eternal plan of salvation. Luke highlights the threefold spread of the gospel through his structure of Luke–Acts and also in specific parables like that of the kingdom banquet in Luke 14. Through his narrative, he communicates to the Gentiles that their salvation, and the apparent rejection of that salvation by the Jews, is within God's plan and control.

In contrast, Paul uses propositions to convince the Jewish believers, and the Gentile converts themselves, that they belong to God's elect people. He indicates that their status is part of the original plan of God which predates the historical calling of the Jews to be God's people. On this basis, Paul can use election and call language to encourage the believers in the face of persecution, temptation, and uncertainty about the Parousia. God has chosen and called them, so the readers should persevere.

CONCLUSIONS

For both Paul and Luke, the fact that Israel was initially offered salvation, but that it is now being offered to the Gentiles as well, is part of God's eternal purpose. Although the genre they use to communicate this truth is different, the language of "call" is a common feature.

Paul and Luke use different language to describe the imperative for Christian transformation, but "call" is again a common thread. Paul says that the call is to be holy or sanctified. Luke says that the call is to repentance (Luke 5:27–32). The concepts are not too far apart. The desire to be holy and sanctified, using Paul's terminology, is a response to being aware of one's call to salvation. Similarly, the desire to repent, using Luke's terminology, which means to not only verbally apologize but also to change one's life, also emerges from an awareness of one's call to salvation. Both are advocating changed behavior as a consequence of call.

Both Luke and Paul also use "call" language in association with the kingdom of God. The kingdom is far more prominent in the Synoptic Gospels, especially its imperative towards ethical behavior. In Luke 14, καλέω is clearly linked to the kingdom through the great messianic banquet. But in the Thessalonian correspondence, Paul also links the kingdom to "call" and draws ethical imperatives.

For both Luke and Paul, the call to salvation supersedes one's ethnic or socioeconomic status. In the parable of the Great Banquet, Luke demonstrates that the social and religious outcasts and even the Gentiles are now the "elect" and the "called." Paul communicates the same truth propositionally in Romans 9 to 11. In 1 Corinthians, he highlights that one's status in life is made irrelevant by God's call. In Galatians, he argues that ethnicity is also irrelevant.

The call of God also involves the individual becoming involved in a community of faith. This emphasis on community sits squarely within the OT understanding of election to salvation. Election is a social concept and it is only rarely that the idea of election is connected with an individual, such as a prophet, and then only for a special task. Admittedly Jesus' use of the messianic covenant banquet as a symbol for salvation comes from OT theology, but it is likely that he and Luke also wished it to convey this message about community to the called. It is the same message that Jesus himself manifests in his own behavior and words in the communal banquet setting. God's salvation is an inclusive communal one. Paul's use of ἐκκλησία, his indication that believers are called into the fellowship of Christ in 1 Corinthians, and his expression in Galatians that believers are called to love and serve one another, suggest that Paul also saw that the call to salvation was a call to community. His metaphors for the church, such as body, would strongly support this assumption.

There are undoubtedly differences in the way that Paul and Luke use καλέω language and the concepts with which they associate with it. However, we have seen that there are also significant points of connection between the two in the usage of this term.

In light of this, translators should reconsider the seemingly arbitrary translation of καλέω into "invite" and "call." Translating the same word as two different English words suggests that there is a dichotomy of meaning where there is in fact a commonality. If "invitation" is used as a translation of καλέω, perhaps a translator's footnote could be used to explain that it could also be translated as "call" to address this false dichotomy.

Much of the heat has gone out of the "Paul founded Christianity" assertion. Still, what we have found about the use of καλέω by Paul and Luke provides evidence for those who are looking for a more consistent soteriology in both. The common use of καλέω brings with it a range of other soteriological concepts such as election, covenant, and sanctification.

6.4 Call and the Christian Life

A greater prominence given to the soteriological category of call emerging from the purposeful use of καλέω by both Paul and Luke suggest implications for Christian life and conduct. The reason for this is that various categories of metaphor for salvation give Christians varying ideas of self-identity. For example, the metaphor of adoption is powerful because it gives a clear illustration of the status of sonship. However, the metaphor of being "called" is also pregnant with meaning. The notion of being called means the Christian is named, summoned, and set apart. Those who were nothing are now part of the people of God. As Christians reflect on the significance of call as a direct descriptor of salvation, so their identity is strengthened, and so their behavior and thought are transformed.

It is remarkable how often "love" is associated with God's calling or election. Those who are called are also "beloved by God" (Rom 1:6–7). The choosing of Jacob is described in terms of God placing his love on him (Rom 9:13). In 1 Thessalonians 1:4, Paul explains the Thessalonian's faith, love, and hope in terms of their election. The Jews are considered loved because of their fathers (Rom 11:28). Clearly, the love expressed by the caller is to be reflected in the life of the called.

More specifically here are the things which believers are called to:

- freedom (Gal 5:13)
- love and service (Gal 5:13)

- kingdom and glory (1 Thess 2:12)
- a life worthy of the calling (Eph 4:1; 1 Thess 2:12; 2 Thess 1:11)
- holiness/sanctification (1 Thess 4:7; 5:24; 1 Cor 1:2; Rom 1:7)
- the fellowship of his Son (1 Cor 1:9)
- hope (Eph 1:18; 4:4)
- peace (1 Cor 7:15; Col 3:15)
- one's present and future walk in life (1 Cor 7:17)
- belong to Jesus Christ (Rom 1:6)
- existence (Rom 4:17)
- justification (Rom 8:30)
- egalitarian community (Luke 14:16–24; Gal 5:13; 1 Cor 1:2, 9)
- the great messianic banquet (Luke 14:12–24).

The list represents both clear guidance and motivation for living a life worthy of the one who is calling.

Another aspect of call which helps enlighten Christian thought and practice is that call is always for a purpose, not an end in itself. Scholars such as Wright[4] and Newbigin[5] have reminded us of an understanding of "call" and "covenant" as first and foremost pointing to a mission in this world. Israel was called in order that it might be a light to the nations. The idea is of being blessed to be a blessing.

Likewise, Christians are called not for the sake of it, but for the purpose of proclaiming the gospel. Like election, calling involves both privilege and responsibility. The concept of call suggests both invitation and vocation. In Galatians 1:16, Paul writes that when it pleased God to reveal his son to him it was "so that I might proclaim among the Gentiles." Similarly, believers are called so as to call others to the banquet of the Lamb. Thus, the few are called to call the many.

Metaphors of salvation, such as justification by faith, can result in a Christian stagnation. The implications and setting of salvation are entirely "otherworldly"—often in a cosmological courtroom. However, "call" as the metaphor of salvation is far more active. The call implies a "caller" who is impelling the one called towards a mission. As such, call as a soteriological category can go some way to addressing the idea that once you become a

---

4. Wright, *The Mission of God: Unlocking the Bible's Grand Narrative*.
5. Newbigin, *The Open Secret: An Introduction to the Theory of Mission*.

Christian all you need to do is wait until you die to receive heaven. A sense of call means that there is something to do in this world right now.

It should also be noted that Christian calling is primarily a communal one. Many categories of soteriology can be interpreted individualistically. However, plural language dominates election and call texts. Paul has conceived of election and call in the NT in terms similar to the election of Israel. As Israel became God's chosen people when God chose Abraham, so the church finds her election in solidarity with Christ and his election.[6] Further, the corporate nature of God's call on those who were "not a people" to become "the people of God" has implications for the corporate nature of the Christian life. As the soteriological category of call has a greater place in the Christian mindset, so does one's corporate understanding of salvation. The theologically informed, and celebrated, concept of Christian call inherently compels Christians towards community where there is no division according to socioeconomic or ethnic lines. We can no longer only say "God chose me." We must have the understanding that "God called us."

Guinness,[7] quoting Havel, says the notion of calling is vital to each of us because it touches on the modern search for a basis for individual identity and an understanding of humanness itself. He argues that all attempts to explain human individuality in general terms can be summed up as varieties of:

1. Constrained to be (we become prisoners of our category, be it gender, class, race, generation, or ancestry).
2. Courage to be (we all have the freedom to be whatever we want to be).
3. Constituted to be (we carry the script of our life stories).
4. Called to be.

To some extent we are all "constrained to be." An understanding of the many forces shaping us is invaluable. We must also have the "courage to be" if we are truly to be ourselves and not prisoners of our past and victims of our circumstances. And to a certain extent the "courage to be" will lie along the trajectory of what we are "constituted to be." But all three pale into insignificance when compared to the fourth understanding of identity which generates the wonder and truth of calling.

The caller sees and addresses us as individuals—as unique, exceptional, precious, significant, and free to respond. He who calls us is personal as

---

6. Klein, *The New Chosen People: A Corporate View of Election*, 264.

7. Guinness, *The Call: Finding and Fulfilling the Central Purpose of Your Life*, 20–23.

well as infinite. We are called and addressed as individuals and invited into relationship—"I have called you by name. You are mine." Responding to the call requires courage, but we are not on our own. It means rising to a challenge, but in partnership and in intimate relationship with the caller and the fellow called. Following his call, we become what we are constituted to be in creation. We also become what we are not yet, and can only become, by re-creation as a called people. Yet human identity is neither fixed nor final. It is incomplete. As such, we can refuse the call and remained stunted. Or we may respond to the call and rise to become the magnificent creatures that only the caller can call us to be.

Bibliography

Allen, Leslie C. "Romans." In *New International Bible Commentary*, edited by F. F. Bruce. Grand Rapids: Zondervan, 1970.
Anderson, Bernhard Word, and Steven Bishop. *The Contours of Old Testament Theology*. Minneapolis: Fortress, 1999.
Arndt, Danker, et al. *A Greek–English Lexicon of the New Testament and Other Early Christian Literature*. 3rd ed. Chicago: University of Chicago Press, 2000.
Babylonian Talmud Shabbath 153a.
Bailey, Kenneth E. *Through Peasant Eyes: A Literary-Cultural Approach to the Parables in Luke*. Grand Rapids: Eerdmans, 1983.
Bailey, Mark L. "Guidelines for Interpreting Jesus' Parables." *Bibliotheca Sacra* 155, no. 617 (1998): 29–38.
Baltzer, Klaus. *The Covenant Formulary in Old Testament, Jewish and Early Christian Writings*. Oxford: Blackwell, 1971.
Barr, James. *The Semantics of Biblical Language*. Oxford: Oxford University Press, 1978.
Barrett, Charles Kingsley. *A Commentary on the Epistle to the Romans*. London: A. and C. Black, 1957.
Bauckham, Richard J. *2 Peter, Jude*. Word Biblical Commentary. Vol. 50. Dallas: Word, 1998.
Beale, Gregory K., and Donald A. Carson. *Commentary on the New Testament Use of the Old Testament*. Grand Rapids: Baker Academic, 2007.
Beker, Johan Christiaan. *Paul the Apostle: The Triumph of God in Life and Thought*. Philadelphia: Fortress, 1980.
Berger, Klaus. "Jesus Als Pharisäer Und Frühe Christen Als Pharisäer." *Novum Testamentum* 30, no. 3 (1988): 231–62.
Berkhof, Louis. *Systematic Theology*. Edinburgh: Banner of Truth Trust, 1958.
Bird, Michael F. *Introducing Paul: The Man, His Mission and His Message*. Downers Grove: IVP Academic, 2009.
———. "Introduction." In *Paul and the Gospels: Christologies, Conflicts, and Convergences*, edited by M. F. Bird and J. Willitts. New York: T. & T. Clark, 2011.
———. "Justification as Forensic Declaration and Covenant Membership: A *Via Media* between Reformed and Revisionist Readings of Paul." *Tyndale Bulletin* 57, no. 1 (2006): 109–30.
Boice, James Montgomery. "Galatians." In *The Expositor's Bible Commentary*, edited by Frank E. Gaebelein. Grand Rapids: Zondervan, 1976.

Borgen, Peder. "From Paul to Luke: Observations toward Clarification of the Theology of Luke–Acts." *Catholic Biblical Quarterly* 31 (1969): 168–82.
Braun, Willi. *Feasting and Social Rhetoric in Luke 14*. Cambridge: Cambridge University Press, 2005.
Bruce, Frederick F. *1 and 2 Thessalonians*. Word Biblical Commentary. Vol. 45. Dallas: Word, 1998.
Calvin, John. "Genesis." In *The Geneva Series of Commentaries*. Edited and translated by John King. 1847. Edinburgh: The Banner of Truth Trust, 1965.
Campbell, William S. "Covenant and New Covenant." In *Dictionary of Paul and His Letters*, edited by G. F. Hawthorne et al., 179–83. Downers Grove, IL: InterVarsity, 1993.
Carson, Donald A. "Matthew." In *The Expositor's Bible Commentary: Matthew, Mark, Luke*, edited by Frank E. Gaebelein. Grand Rapids: Zondervan, 1984.
Carson, France, et al. *New Bible Commentary: 21st Century Edition*. 4th ed. Leicester: InterVarsity, 1994.
Chester, Stephen J. *Conversion at Corinth*. London: T. &. T. Clark, 2003.
Cho, Youngmo. "Spirit and Kingdom in Luke–Acts: Proclamation as the Primary Role of the Spirit in Relation to the Kingdom of God in Luke–Acts." *Asian Journal of Pentecostal Studies* 6, no. 2 (2003): 173–97.
Christensen, Duane L. *Deuteronomy 21:10—34:12*. Word Biblical Commentary. Vol. 6b. Dallas: Word, 2002.
Ciampa, Roy E., and Brian S. Rosner. *The First Letter to the Corinthians*. Grand Rapids: Eerdmans, 2010.
Colijn, Brenda B. *Images of Salvation in the New Testament*. Downers Grove: InterVarsity, 2010.
Conzelmann, Hans. *The Theology of St. Luke*. Translated by G. Buswell. London: SCM, 1982.
Crabbe, Kylie. "Transforming Tables: Meals as Encounters with the Kingdom in Luke." Unpublished MTh Thesis., Melbourne College of Divinity, 2010.
Cronshaw, Darren. "Mission as Hosting Community Hospitality in Multicultural Australia." A paper for presentation at the Australian Missiology Conference, Melbourne, 26–30 September, 2005.
Daube, David. *The New Testament and Rabbinic Judaism*. New York: Arno, 1973.
Davies, William David. "Paul: From the Jewish Point of View." In *The Cambridge History of Judaism*, edited by William David Davies et al. Cambridge: Cambridge University Press, 2006.
de Villiers, Pieter. "Soteriological Perspectives in 1 Thessalonians." In *Salvation in the New Testament: Perspectives on Soteriology*, edited by Jan G. van der Watt, 305–29. Leiden: Brill, 2005.
Dennis, L. T., and Wayne A. Grudem. *The ESV Study Bible*. Wheaton: Crossway, 2008.
Doble, Peter. *The Paradox of Salvation: Luke's Theology of the Cross*. Cambridge: Cambridge University Press, 2005.
du Plessis, I. J. "The Saving Significance of Jesus and His Death on the Cross in Luke's Gospel: Focusing on Luke 22:19b-20." *Neotestamentica* 28, no. 2 (1994): 523–40.
Dumbrell, William J. "Justification and the New Covenant." *Churchman* 112 (1998): 17–29.

Duncan, J. Ligon. "Covenant in the Synoptics, Acts and Pauline Writings." http://www.fpcjackson.org/resources/apologetics/covenant%20theology%20&%20justification/ligons_covtheology/11.htm.

Dunn, James D. G. "Did Paul Have a Covenant Theology? Reflections on Romans 9:4 and 11:27." In *The Concept of the Covenant in the Second Temple Period*, edited by Stanley E. Porter and Jacqueline de Roo, 287-307. Leiden: Brill, 2003.

———. "The New Perspective on Paul." *Bulletin of the John Rylands Library* 65 (1983): 95-122.

———. *Romans 1-8*. Word Biblical Commentary. Vol. 38a. Dallas: Word, 1988.

———. *Romans 9-16*. Word Biblical Commentary. Vol. 38b. Dallas: Word, 1988.

———. *The Theology of Paul the Apostle*. Grand Rapids: Eerdmans, 1998.

Eichrodt, Walther. *Theology of the Old Testament*. Vol. 1. Translated by J. A Baker. Philadelphia: Westminster Press, 1961.

Ellis, Edward Earle. *The Gospel of Luke*. London: Nelson, 1966.

Ellison, H. L. "Genesis 1-11." In *New International Bible Commentary*, edited by Frederick F. Bruce, 1316-17. Grand Rapids: Zondervan, 1979.

Erickson, Millard J. *Christian Theology*. Grand Rapids: Baker, 1985.

Eslinger, Lyle. "Prehistory in the Call to Abraham." *Biblical Interpretation* 14 (2006): 189-208.

Evans, Christopher F. *Saint Luke*. London: SCM, 2008.

Evans, Craig A. "Luke's Use of the Elijah/Elisha Narratives and the Ethic of Election." *Journal of Biblical Literature* 106, no. 1 (1987): 75-83.

Fanning, Buist M. "Theological Analysis." In *Interpreting the New Testament Text: Introduction to the Art and Science of Exegesis*, edited by Darrell L. Bock and Buist M. Fanning, 277-91. Wheaton: Crossway, 2006.

Fensham, F. C. "The Covenant as Giving Expression to the Relationship between the Old and New Testament." *Tyndale Bulletin* 22 (1971): 82-94.

Ferguson, Sinclair B., and James I. Packer. *New Dictionary of Theology*. Electronic Ed. Downers Grove: InterVarsity, 2000.

Fitzmyer, Joseph A. *Paul and His Theology: A Brief Sketch*. Englewood Cliffs: Prentice Hall, 1989.

Franklin, Eric. *Christ the Lord: A Study in the Purpose and Theology of Luke-Acts*. Philadelphia: Westminster, 1975.

Fraser, John William. *Jesus and Paul*. Appleford: Marcham, 1974.

Furnish, Victor Paul. "The Jesus-Paul Debate: From Baur to Bultmann." In *Paul and Jesus: Collected Essays*, edited by A. J. M. Wedderburn. London; New York: T. & T. Clark, 2004.

Garlington, Donald. *Studies in the New Perspective on Paul: Essays and Reviews*. Eugene: Wipf & Stock, 2008.

Grams, Rollin G. "Contextualisation, Intertextuality, and Paul's Soteriology." *Transformation* 23, no. 1 (2006): 3-16.

Green, Joel. *The Theology of the Gospel of Luke*. Cambridge: Cambridge University Press, 1995.

Grogan, Geoffrey W. "Isaiah. " In *The Expositor's Bible Commentary, Vol. 6: Isaiah, Jeremiah, Lamentations, Ezekiel*, edited by Frank E. Gaebelein, 255. Grand Rapids: Zondervan, 1986.

Grudem, Wayne A. *Systematic Theology: An Introduction to Biblical Doctrine*. Grand Rapids: InterVarsity, 1994.

Guinness, Os. *The Call: Finding and Fulfilling the Central Purpose of Your Life*. Nashville: Thomas Nelson, 2003.

Guthrie, Donald. *New Testament Introduction*. Leicester: InterVarsity, 1970.

Haenchen, Ernst. *The Acts of the Apostles*. Translated by Gerald Shinn and Bernard Noble. Oxford: Basil Blackwell, 1971.

Halliday, Michael A. K. *Language as Social Semiotic: The Social Interpretation of Language and Meaning*. London: Arnold, 1978.

Harrison, Everett F. "Romans." In *The Expositor's Bible Commentary, Vol. 10: Romans through Galatians*, edited by F. E. Gaebelein. Grand Rapids: Zondervan, 1976.

Hassler, Andrew. "Justification and the Individual in the Wake of the New Perspective on Paul." The Southern Baptist Theological Seminary, 2011.

Hawthorne, Gerald F. *Philippians*. Word Biblical Commentary. Vol. 43. Dallas: Word, 2004.

Hicks, John Mark. "The Lord's Table: A Covenant Meal." *Leaven* 3, no. 3 (2012): 3.

Hoehner, Harold W. "Ephesians." In *The Bible Knowledge Commentary: An Exposition of the Scriptures*, Vol. 2, edited by J. F. Walvoord and R. B. Zuck. Wheaton: Victor, 1985.

Hoehner, Comfort, et al. *Cornerstone Biblical Commentary: Ephesians, Philippians, Colossians, 1 & 2 Thessalonians, Philemon*. Vol. 16. Carol Stream: Tyndale House, 2008.

Homer. *The Iliad*. Edited by Courtland Canby. Translated by Samuel Butler. Geneva: Heron, 1969.

Hussey, Ian. "The Soteriological Use of 'Call' in the New Testament: An Undervalued Category?". *Biblical Theology Bulletin: Journal of Bible and Culture* 46, no. 3 (2016): 133–43.

Hutchins, Robert M. ed. *Great Books of the Western World, Vol. 7: Plato*. Chicago: Encyclopaedia Britannica, 1952.

Jackson, Donald. "Luke and Paul: A Theology of One Spirit from Two Perspectives." *Journal of the Evangelical Theological Society* 32, no. 3 (1989): 336–54.

Jeremias, Joachim. *The Eucharistic Words of Jesus*. London: SCM, 1966.

Keener, Craig S. *The IVP Bible Background Commentary: New Testament*. Electronic ed. Downers Grove: InterVarsity, 1993.

Keifert, Patrick R. *Welcoming the Stranger*. Minneapolis: Fortress, 1992.

Kilgallen, John J. "A Major Difference between Law and Faith, in Luke and His Traditions." *Expository Times* 116, no. 2 (2004): 37–41.

Klein, William. *The New Chosen People: A Corporate View of Election*. Grand Rapids: Academie, 1990.

———. "Paul's Use of Kalein: A Proposal." *Journal of the Evangelical Theological Society* 27 (1984): 53–64.

Koehler, Baumgartner, et al. *The Hebrew and Aramaic Lexicon of the Old Testament*. Leiden; New York: E. J. Brill, 1999.

Koenig, J. "Occasions of Grace in Paul, Luke and First Century Judaism." *Anglican Theological Review* 64, no. 4 (1982): 562–76.

Kovács, Frank Zoltan. "The Covenant Concept as an Organising Principle in Luke–Acts." PhD diss., North-West University, 2011.

———. "The Covenant in Luke–Acts." Unpublished MTh Thesis; North-West University, South Africa, 2006.

Kümmel, Werner Georg. *Introduction to the New Testament*. London: SCM, 1975.

Larkin, William J. "Luke's Use of the Old Testament as a Key to His Soteriology." *Journal of the Evangelical Theological Society* 20 (1977): 325-35.
Leifeld, Walter L. "Luke." In *The Expositor's Bible Commentary, Vol. 8: Matthew, Mark, Luke*, edited by Frank E. Gaebelein, 809-15. Grand Rapids: Zondervan, 1984.
Lillback, Peter A. "Covenant." In *New Dictionary of Theology*, edited by S. Ferguson et al. Downers Grove: InterVarsity, 1987.
Lincoln, Andrew T. *Ephesians*. Word Biblical Commentary. Vol. 42. Dallas: Word, 1990.
Lodge, John G. "The Salvation Theologies of Paul and Luke." *Chicago Studies* 22, no. 1 (1983): 35-52.
Longenecker, Richard N. "The Acts of the Apostles." In *The Expositor's Bible Commentary, Vol. 9: John and Acts*, edited by Frank E. Gaebelein. Grand Rapids: Zondervan, 1981.
———. *Galatians*. Word Biblical Commentary. Vol. 41. Dallas: Word, 1998.
Louw, Johannes P., and Eugene Albert Nida. *Greek-English Lexicon of the New Testament: Based on Semantic Domains*. Vol. 2. New York: United Bible Societies, 1988.
Lowery, David K. "1 Corinthians." In *The Bible Knowledge Commentary: An Exposition of the Scriptures*, edited by J. F. Walvoord and R. B. Zuck. Wheaton: Victor, 1985.
Lyons, John. *Introduction to Theoretical Linguistics*. Cambridge: Cambridge University Press, 1968.
MacDonald, Nathan. *Not Bread Alone: The Uses of Food in the Old Testament*. Oxford: Oxford University Press, 2008.
Mare, W. Harold. "1 Corinthians." In *The Expositor's Bible Commentary, Vol. 10: Romans through Galatians*, edited by Frank E. Gaebelein. Grand Rapids: Zondervan, 1976.
Marsh, Paul W. "1 Corinthians." In *New International Bible Commentary*, edited by F. F. Bruce. Grand Rapids: Zondervan, 1979.
Marshall, I. Howard. "2 Thessalonians." In *New Bible Commentary: 21st Century Edition*, edited by D. A. Carson et al. Leicester: InterVarsity, 1994.
———. *Commentary on Luke*. New International Greek Testament Commentary. Grand Rapids: Eerdmans, 1978.
———. "Election and Calling to Salvation in 1 and 2 Thessalonians." In *The Thessalonian Correspondence*, edited by Raymond F. Collins, 259-76. Leuven: Leuven University Press, 1988.
———. *Luke: Historian and Theologian*. Leicester: InterVarsity, 1998.
Martin, Ralph P. *Ephesians, Colossians and Philemon*. Louisville: Westminster John Knox, 2012.
———. "Salvation and Discipleship in Luke's Gospel." *Interpretation* 30, no. 4 (1976): 366-80.
Matthews, Chavalas, et al. "Genesis 17:3-8." In *The IVP Bible Background Commentary: Old Testament*. Electronic Ed. Downers Grove: InterVarsity, 2000.
McIver, Robert K. "Pauline Images of Salvation." *Ministry Magazine* (1991).
Merriam-Webster Dictionary. "Call." Encyclopaedia Britannica. http://www.merriam-webster.com/dictionary/call.
———. "Invite." Encyclopaedia Britannica. http://www.merriam-webster.com/dictionary/invite.
Mohrlang, Roger, and Gerald L. Borchert. *Cornerstone Biblical Commentary, Vol 14: Romans and Galatians*. Carol Stream: Tyndale House, 2007.
Moo, Douglas J. *The New International Commentary on the New Testament: The Epistle to the Romans*. Grand Rapids: Eerdmans, 1996.

Morlan, David Scott. "Conversion in Luke and Paul: Some Exegetical and Theological Explorations." Unpublished Doctoral Dissertation; Durham University, 2010.

Morris, Leon. *The First Epistle of Paul to the Corinthians: An Introduction and Commentary*. Tyndale New Testmant Commentaries. Vol. 7. Grand Rapids: Eerdmans, 1985.

———. "Salvation." In *Dictionary of Paul and His Letters*, edited by G. F. Hawthorne et al., 858-62. Downers Grove: InterVarsity, 1993.

Newbigin, Lesslie. *The Open Secret: An Introduction to the Theory of Mission*. Grand Rapids: Eerdmans, 1995.

Nolland, John. *Luke 1:1—9:20*. Word Biblical Commentary. Vol. 35a. Dallas: Word, 2002.

O'Brien, Peter T. *Colossians, Philemon*. Word Biblical Commentary. Vol. 44. Dallas: Word, 1998.

Osborne, Grant R. *The Hermeneutical Spiral: A Comprehensive Introduction to Biblical Interpretation*. Downers Grove: InterVarsity, 2006.

Payne, David F. "Isaiah." In *New International Bible Commentary*, edited by F. F. Bruce. Grand Rapids: Zondervan, 1979.

Peterson, D. G. "Holiness." In *New Dictionary of Biblical Theology*, edited by Desmond Alexander and Brian S. Rosner. Downers Grove: InterVarsity, 2000.

Piper, John. *The Future of Justification: A Response to N. T. Wright*. Wheaton: Crossway, 2007.

Pitre, Brant. "Jesus, the Messianic Banquet, and the Kingdom of God." In *Liturgy and Empire: Faith in Exile and Political Theology*, edited by Scott Hahn and David Scott, 144-66. Steubenville, Ohio: Emmaus Road, 2009.

Porter, Stanley E. "The Concept of Covenant in Paul." In *The Concept of the Covenant in the Second Temple Period*, edited by Stanley E. Porter and Jacqueline de Roo, 269-85. Leiden: Brill, 2003.

———. "Luke: Companion or Disciple of Paul." In *Paul and the Gospels: Christologies, Conflicts, and Convergences*, edited by Michael F. Bird and Joel Willitts, 146-68. London: T. & T. Clark, 2011.

Powell, Mark Allan. *Introducing the New Testament: A Historical, Literary, and Theological Survey*. Grand Rapids: Baker Academic, 2009.

———. "Salvation in Luke-Acts." *Word & World* 12, no. 1 (1992): 5-10.

Quell, G. "Ἐκλέγομαι." Translated by G. W. Bromiley. In *Theological Dictionary of the New Testament*, Vol. 4, edited by Friedrich Kittel, 140-54. Grand Rapids: Eerdmans, 1989.

Reardon, Timothy W. "Recent Trajectories and Themes in Lukan Soteriology." *Currents in Biblical Research* 12, no. 1 (2013): 77-95.

Rees, T. "Children of God." In *International Standard Bible Encyclopaedia*, edited by James Orr. Grand Rapids: Eerdmans, 1939.

Robert B. Chisholm Jr. "Hosea." In *The Bible Knowledge Commentary: An Exposition of the Scriptures*, Vol. 1, edited by J. F. Walvoord and R. B. Zuck. Wheaton: Victor, 1985.

Robinson, J. A. *Commentary on Ephesians*. London: Macmillan, 1903.

Ryken, Phillip G. *Justification*. Wheaton: Crossway, 2011.

Ryken, Wilhoit, et al. *Dictionary of Biblical Imagery*. InterVarsity: Downers Grove, 2000.

Ryrie, C. C. *Basic Theology: A Popular Systemic Guide to Understanding Biblical Truth*. Chicago: Moody, 1999.

Sanders, E. P. *Paul and Palestinian Judaism: A Comparison of Patterns of Religion*. Philadelphia: Fortress, 1977.

———. *Paul, the Law, and the Jewish People*. Philadelphia: Fortress, 1983.

Sanders, James A. "The Ethic of Election in Luke's Great Banquet Parable." In *Essays in Old Testament Ethics*, edited by James L. Crenshaw and John T. Willis, 246–71. New York: KTAV, 1974.

Schmidt, K. L. "Καλέω." Translated by G. W. Bromiley. In *Theological Dictionary of the New Testament*, Vol. 3, edited by Friedrich Kittel, 487–91. Grand Rapids: Eerdmans, 1989.

Schreiner, Thomas R. *Romans*. Baker Exegetical Commentary on the New Testament. Grand Rapids: Baker Academic, 1998.

Shedd, Russell Philip. *Man in Community*. London: Epworth, 1958.

Silva, Moisés. *New International Dictionary of New Testament Theology and Exegesis*. Vol. 2. 2nd ed. Grand Rapids: Zondervan, 2014.

Smith, William Robertson. *Lectures on the Religion of the Semites: The Fundamental Institutions*. London: A. & C. Black, 1927.

Stein, Robert H. "Last Supper." In *Dictionary of Jesus and the Gospels.*, edited by J. B. Green et al., 445. Downers Grove: InterVarsity, 1992.

———. *Luke*. The New American Commentary. Nashville: Broadman & Holman, 1992.

Swanson, James. *Dictionary of Biblical Languages with Semantic Domains: Hebrew (Old Testament)*. Oak Harbor: Logos Research Systems, 1997.

Taeger, Jens W. "Paulus Und Lukas Über Den Menschen." *Zeitschrift für die neutestamentliche Wissenschaft und die Kunde der älteren Kirche* 71, no. 1 (1980): 96–108.

Talbert, Charles H. "Shifting Sands: The Recent Study of the Gospel of Luke." *Interpretation* 30, no. 4 (1976): 381–95.

Theissen, Gerd. "Soteriologische Symbolik in Den Paulinischen Schriften." *Kerygma und Dogma* 20 (1974): 282–304.

Thiselton, Anthony C. "Semantics and New Testament Interpretation." In *New Testament Interpretation*, edited by I. H. Marshall, 75–104. Exeter: Paternoster, 1977.

Thomas, Robert L. "2 Thessalonians." In *The Expositor's Bible Commentary, Vol. 11: Ephesians through Philemon*, edited by Frank E. Gaebelein. Grand Rapids: Zondervan 1981.

Toussaint, Stanley D. "Acts." In *The Bible Knowledge Commentary: An Exposition of the Scriptures*, edited by J. F. Walvoord and R. B. Zuck. Wheaton: Victor, 1985.

Trites, Allison A., and William J. Larkin. *The Gospel of Luke and Acts*. Cornerstone Biblical Commentary. Vol. 12. Carol Stream: Tyndale, 2006.

Utley, Robert James. "Paul Bound, the Gospel Unbound: Letters from Prison (Colossians, Ephesians and Philemon, Then Later, Philippians)." Marshall: Bible Lessons International, 1997.

———. "Romans 1:7." In *The Gospel According to Paul: Romans*. Marshall: Bible Lessons International, 1998.

van der Watt, Jan G. *Salvation in the New Testament: Perspectives on Soteriology*. Leiden: Brill, 2005.

van Zyl, Hermie C. "The Soteriological Meaning of Jesus' Death in Luke–Acts: A Survey of Possibilities." *Verbum et Ecclesia* 23, no. 2 (2002): 533–57. http://www.ve.org.za/index.php/VE/article/view/1223.

Vine, W. E. *Vine's Complete Expository Dictionary of Old and New Testament Words*. Nashville: Thomas Nelson, 1996.

Watts, John D. W. *Isaiah 34–66*. Word Biblical Commentary. Vol. 25. Nashville: Thomas Nelson, 2005.

Wenham, David. *Paul: Follower of Jesus or Founder of Christianity?* Grand Rapids: Eerdmans, 1995.

Wenham, David, and Steve Walton. *Exploring the New Testament. Vol. 1: The Gospels and Acts*. 2nd ed. London: Society for Promoting Christian Knowledge, 2011.

Wenham, Gordon J. *Genesis 16–50*. Word Biblical Commentary. Vol. 2. Dallas: Word, 1998.

Witmer, John A. "Romans 9:6–9." In *The Bible Knowledge Commentary: An Exposition of the Scriptures*, edited by John F. Walvoord and Roy B. Zuck. Wheaton: Victor, 1985.

Wood, A. Skevington. "Ephesians." In *The Expositor's Bible Commentary: Ephesians through Philemon*, Vol. 11, edited by Frank E. Gaebelein. Grand Rapids: Zondervan, 1981.

Wrede, William. *Paul*. London: Green, 1907.

Wright, Christopher J. H. *The Mission of God: Unlocking the Bible's Grand Narrative*. Leicester: IVP Academic, 2006.

Wright, Nicholas Thomas. *Paul: In Fresh Perspective*. London: SPCK, 2005.

———. "The Paul of History and the Apostle of Faith." *Tyndale Bulletin* 29 (1978): 61–88.

———. *What Saint Paul Really Said*. Oxford: Lion, 1997.

www.ingramcontent.com/pod-product-compliance
Lightning Source LLC
Chambersburg PA
CBHW071448160426
43195CB00013B/2051